Relax Focus Succeed®

A Guide to Balancing Your Personal and Professional Lives and Becoming More Successful in Both

by
Karl W. Palachuk

Published by

Great Little Book Publishing

Sacramento, CA
Phone 800-822-3585
www.GreatLittleBook.com

Great Little Book Publishing
2121 Natomas Crossing Dr., #200
Sacramento, CA 95834

Relax Focus Succeed®: *A Guide to Balancing Your Personal and Professional Lives and Becoming More Successful in Both*
Copyright © 2007 by Karl W. Palachuk

Some parts of this book were derived from articles originally published on the web site www.RelaxFocusSucceed.com.

ISBN 10: 0-9763760-0-8
ISBN 13: 978-0-9763760-0-2

www.greatlittlebook.com

Printed in the United States of America
5 4 3 2 1

This book is dedicated to everyone out there seeking a happy, healthy, fulfilling life. None of us is free from adversity. But once you commit yourself to being successful, no obstacle can stand in your way.

– KP

Contents

Foreword

I'm very pleased to write a foreword for Karl Palachuk's latest book, Relax Focus Succeed.

As a sales trainer and author, I meet lots of people who are eager to do "whatever it takes" to move to a higher level of effectiveness. Karl's book is exactly the tool they're looking for. We all dream. Karl shows us how to dream elaborately. We all set goals. Karl shows us how to set goals that make our lives more fulfilling.

From the world of sales I can tell you, there two great impediments to success in the modern work world. The first is not having goals to which you can hold yourself (and your team) accountable. The second is stress, which most often comes from having too much to do and not enough time to do it. In Relax Focus Succeed we learn that both of these have one cause – lack of focus.

But the lack of focus is not merely a lack of goals. Some people accept goals from others (for example the salesperson who simply accepts a monthly or quarterly challenge). Others set goals but don't make any real commitment to them. These people have goals, but they don't have much reason to achieve them.

Karl does a great job of demonstrating that your goals need to be personal, and your business goals need to be related to your personal goals. Rather than having a "you at work" and a "you at home," you'll just have one you with goals for work and goals for home. That reduces stress and helps you align the roles you play.

If you follow through with the exercises outlined by Karl, you're guaranteed to be successful! You'll be fulfilled at work, fulfilled at home, and fulfilled as a person. Perhaps for the first time in your life, you'll have a "big picture" view of your own life.

As Karl says, this is hard work. You need to take it seriously. But the rewards are amazing and everlasting. Get started today!

All the best!

BFG3

Ben Gay III
www.bfg3.com

About the Author

Karl W. Palachuk is the founder and author of the Relax Focus Succeed® web site (www.relaxfocussucceed.com) and the Relax Focus Succeed® newsletter.

Karl is also the president of KPEnterprises Business Consulting, Inc. and Great Little Book Publishing Co., Inc., both of which he founded. He is involved with, or serves on the boards of, several professional associations and is the author of three books for small business consultants. Karl maintains a mailing list and a blog for technical consultants. In addition, he maintains several web sites that provide resources to these consultants.

Karl has been a featured speaker at conferences and seminars over the last ten years. He is a motivational speaker and trainer on business and technology. He has spoken at several events in Europe and the United Kingdom, as well as in dozens of cities in the United States.

Karl lives in Sacramento, CA with his wife Laura and their daughter Victoria.

About Relax Focus Succeed®

As you will discover inside this book, the concept of Relax Focus Succeed® was borne out of Karl's personal experience in dealing with adversity and building a business at the same time.

While the concepts of balance, hard word, and focus are well established in the "self help" literature, this book combines these fundamental elements with quite a different twist. The emphasis on relaxation actually turns off many people. They just can't get past the belief that digging in and working harder *has to* make them more successful.

The premise of Relax Focus Succeed® is simple but powerful: The fundamental keys to success are Focus, Hard Work, and Balance. Common business advice is full of focus and hard work, but shy on emphasizing balance.

Without relaxation, work cannot be successful. *You* cannot be successful without balancing work and relaxation. Sometimes you have to **not** work. Sometimes you have to give yourself the gift of enjoying your life. And when you do this, consciously aware that you're giving yourself this gift, then you achieve clarity: Your focus becomes sharper, your work more meaningful, and your success that much closer.

Good luck with your journey.

Who Should Read this Book?

This book is useful for everyone who seeks to be happier and more fulfilled. Individuals will find ways to bring harmony between the "roles" they play at home, at work, and in the community. Bosses and managers will find ways to motivate and inspire their workers.

Everyone will gain a better understanding of the linkages that exist between the various complicated aspects of our modern lives.

We each need a plan for our lives, but planning, scheming, and setting goals seems like just more work. In our busy lives, we don't have time to make time to do the things we know we need to do. It's like we don't have time to fix the roof because we're too busy mopping the floor.

In this little book you'll find the key ingredients you'll need to stop, sit down, and begin building a happier, healthier, more balanced and successful life.

There are no magic pills here. You have to do all the work. But the work doesn't have to be unpleasant at all. Everyone can and should work to have a more fulfilling and balanced life.

And this book will show you how to get started.

Acknowledgements

In my previous three books, I had a long list of people to thank. This book is a little different. This book has been incubating for about two years while I did other things.

As strange as it sounds, I thank the Lord for giving me physical challenges in my life that forced me to get off the "fast track" and figure out how to succeed without working fifty or sixty hours a week.

I thank my parents, Frank and Ramona Palachuk, for inspiring me and giving me the confidence to try new things. I thank my wife Laura for putting up with me, and for sticking in there when my physical body gave out.

And I thank all the RFS™ subscribers who gave me so much positive feedback over the years. Without you, I would never have taken the chance to put this all into book form.

On the practical side of putting together a book, I thank Jennifer Corry, my publishing assistant. She has been a great blessing to me and all my businesses for the last couple of years. And while she never saw the first draft of this book, the final draft wouldn't be complete without her.

Finally, I thank Stephanie Martindale for doing the book layout. This is the third book we've done together. As you can imagine, this was the least stressful of the three <wink>.

If I forgot anyone, please forgive me.

– Karl W. Palachuk
Sacramento, CA

Section I:

Introduction and Overview

Thank you for beginning this journey with me.

As the weeks and months and years go by, I am constantly amazed at the tremendous human potential that exists in every one of us. Most people don't spend much time looking within themselves or planning for a more successful future. But those who do soon discover that a better future is easily within their reach.

One of the great "secrets" of success is that almost anything you do consistently over time will bring success. The mere fact that you put your time and energy on a project improves its chances of success. We call that *focus*.

And if *you* are the project, then focusing on *your success* will virtually guarantee it.

There are many paths to success. This book outlines a process that has worked for me. I wrote the book because I believe it will work for you, too.

Focus means more than merely putting a little attention on something for a short period of time. You can turn on a light and see what's in a room. Or you can focus a light and experience greater power. Telescopes focus light and let us see things millions of miles away. Microscopes focus light and show us amazing things in tiny little spaces. Lasers focus light and perform miraculous surgeries that no one dreamed of a few years ago.

Putting some attention on your personal and professional success will move you to be more successful. Focusing on your success – consistently over time – will propel you to greater success in a shorter amount of time.

Focusing on your success is literally like a super power. All you have to do is to exercise that power and channel your energy.

This book starts with some introduction to the Relax Focus Succeed® philosophy. It moves quickly to a discussion about balance and working too hard. Don't misunderstand: You will have to work very hard for your success. There are no magic pills or mantras.

But you also have to play. You have to take time to *not work*. You need to "have a life," as they say. Yet another secret of success is this: Without balance between your personal and professional lives, there is no success.

A billionaire with no personal interests or meaningful relationships is not successful. A workaholic whose family doesn't recognize him is not successful. Being fabulously successful means having great personal relationships, a fulfilling life – and being successful on your job.

You may be asking "How do I do all that at once?" You work at it. Consistently over time. You focus like a laser beam. You create a plan for a balanced life and then proceed to make it come true.

Sound exciting? Then let's get started!

Chapter 1

Relax Focus Succeed®

Introduction

One Fall morning I woke up and couldn't get out of bed. I was tired – exhausted, really. But this was more than that.

My hands and feet hurt. My joints ached. Maybe it was the flu.

I had every reason to be tired – exhausted, really.

My business was growing but seemed to need more attention every day. My family was moving from one house to another and I had to prep the new house in the evenings. When we moved, I spent all my time converting the old house into a rental unit.

All the work on the houses took time away from my business. So I made the same mistake most sole proprietors would make: I did the work that needed my attention right now and I didn't do the marketing that was needed to bring new work in the door.

It was an extremely stressful, busy, and not very profitable time.

It took me awhile to get out of bed that day. I wrote it off to fatigue and stress. The next day was better, but after that it got worse.

Over the course of three months I went from very healthy to totally exhausted all day, constant pain, and unable to get out of bed in the morning. Eventually, it took me an hour from the time I woke up to muster the strength needed to climb out of bed.

After several trips to the doctor I was finally diagnosed with Rheumatoid Arthritis, an immune disease in which the body attacks itself. Basically, the immune system goes into overload. While some people get R.A. at a young age, it most commonly attacks people in their late 30's or early 40's. I was 39.

Once I was properly diagnosed, I went through a series of horrible drug treatments. It would be years before I could function normally again. And it would be many years before I accepted the fact that I will never have another day without pain as long as I live.

But that's not the good part of the story!

Somewhere in those years, I grew my company, started two other businesses, wrote three books, and became wealthy by most peoples' standards. More importantly, I was personally happy and fulfilled, my marriage was strong, and our daughter was a happy, well-balanced kid.

This transition is not a coincidence. Quite the contrary. It is from the depths of my illness that I discovered the formula for personal and professional success.

This book was written to help you find the same path – without the chronic disease! I don't mean a path to money, but a path of true success: of happiness, fulfillment, and balance.

> It is from the depths of my illness that I discovered the formula for personal and professional success.

I hope that, in these pages, you'll dedicate yourself to building the future you say you want.

Wishing for Success

Most of us use the word "wish" in a way that is truly meaningless.

- I wish I had better family relationships.

- I wish I could play the piano.

- I wish I had more money.

- I wish my office weren't so messy.

- I wish I had more time with the kids.

- I wish my spouse and I had more romance.

- I wish . . . I wish . . . I wish.

It is always easier to see what other people should be doing differently. So let's go there first. Think about someone you know who says "I wish." Imagine yourself asking that person "So what have you been doing about it?"

"You say you want to be better at _____. What have you been doing about it? Have you taken a class? Bought a book? Bought the right tools? Spent an hour a day working on it?"

"No?" you'll ask your friend. "You say you wish this, but you've done nothing about it."

Let's not be too hard on your friend. Why? Well, because you're next. What do you wish for? And what have you done about it?

Do you wish like a child? Do you close your eyes and imagine that one day you'll have everything you want? Or do you wish like an adult, with your eyes open, pencil in hand, ready to take visible action to make your dream come true?

The bad news is: you're all grown up now and you have to create every good thing in your life. You have to decide what you want, and you have to work toward it.

But there's good news, too.

The good news is, true success is easily within your grasp and much more spectacular than you imagined it to be. Success includes love, happiness, health, and money if you want it.

But you need to wish with your eyes open and a pencil in your hand.

The Philosophy

My premise is simple but powerful: I believe the fundamental keys to success are Focus, Hard Work, and Balance. "Success literature" is full of Focus and Hard Work but shy on emphasizing Balance. Two notable exceptions are Wayne Dyer and Og Mandino.

Without Relaxation, without balance, work cannot be successful. You cannot be successful without balance. Sometimes you have to not work. Sometimes you have to give yourself the gift of enjoying your life. And when you do this, consciously aware that you're giving yourself this gift, then you achieve clarity: Your Focus becomes sharper, your work more meaningful, and your Success that much closer.

I place Relax first because it is the most important and most neglected element. Only when you learn to relax and bring balance to your life will you be truly successful.

Focus is second because it is the driving force in everything we do and everything we achieve. If you focus on watching television, you master watching television; if you focus on your children you will be an excellent parent; if you focus on money you will attain money; if you focus on being a better person, you become a better person.

And if you want to be an excellent parent with enough money to send your kids to college and retire without worrying about paying the bills? Then we're back to Balance – learning to relax and bring the competing elements of your life together in harmony.

The unspoken element is Hard Work. This is not in the title because it's the one element everyone should know about.

I say "should." Unsuccessful people think they can attain their goals without working. They believe they can get rich quick, read a book and straighten out their relationships in an afternoon, or lose weight by taking a sugar pill. I suspect these are the same people who buy hair in a spray can and order diet cola with their super-sized Mondo Burger.

The final element is Success. Success is not money, although having money is one kind of success on which we frequently focus. Success is attaining your goals. Money is often a means to attaining goals, but reflection will tell us that money is never a goal unto itself. Money helps us take vacations, buy toys, enjoy our hobbies, lavish gifts on the people we love, take time for ourselves, contribute to our communities, and attain our goals.

> Success is attaining your goals.

It takes relaxation – and focus – to create and understand the balance in our lives. Relaxation and Focus are absolutely essential to the process of defining, seeking, and attaining our goals. In other words, without relaxation and focus there is no success.

The Origins of Relax Focus Succeed®

So there I was. Having a tough time on my job. Managing a rental house "on the side." Tired all the time. In pain.

As you can imagine, I couldn't exercise much. I used to play racquetball. I realized – six months after being properly diagnosed – that the first sign of my arthritis was losing the ability to grip a racquet for a power shot.

So one day my wife finds out about a program at the local Kaiser hospital. It involves learning meditation as a way to reduce pain. Sounded a little whacko, but the doctor running the class seemed pretty normal. After all, Kaiser's a large medical facility and not some hack shop selling secret potions imported from a third world country.

I went to the class and discovered that other people were there for other reasons. Some people had been referred there to learn simple meditation in order to reduce stress. Okay, I thought, that makes sense.

We all got comfortable, closed our eyes, and the doctor walked us through a simple one minute breathing exercise. Then a two minute exercise, three minute exercise, etc. I now know that this was a simple mindfulness meditation: We focused only on our breath as it moved in and out. All other thoughts were dismissed.

What I discovered was an *increase* in pain. The doctor explained a couple of things. First, this is because I was focused on my breathing and not blocking the pain. I realized that I had come to take pain for granted and had therefore unconsciously set about blocking the pain.

Second, he explained that meditation would eventually help me to realize the boundaries and limits of my pain. In some sense, I would accept it, not fear it, not block it, and simply not focus on it. This was harder to understand.

I started meditating every day.

I had one tape and I listened to it over and over. Then I got a set of tape meditations for pain.

I started a routine:

- Settling in for quiet time.

- 10-15 minutes meditation.

- Quiet time. Not quite meditation, but sitting, thinking, writing down my thoughts.

Eventually, I developed a routine that included meditation, reading, and writing every day.

The thoughts that came to me in my quiet time were all over the map. One day it was my family. Another day work. One day my problems, the next marketing ideas.

Soon I began to realize that my mind was filled with so many thoughts that I could never get them down on paper. Just as our bodies instinctively block pain, they also block our minds from considering every idea or thought that passes through our brains.

We all have thousands – maybe millions – of ideas filling our brains. Most of them are meaningless. Most will never come to anything. But there are gems in there, too. And there are thoughts and ideas that seem unrelated, but don't have to be unrelated. They're like a puzzle. You have to twist them around in your mind to see if they fit, or if there's a piece missing.

Within a year I was spending two or three hours a day in "quiet time." I was reading more, writing more, exercising more, meditating more. I was also exercising more and experiencing less pain.

And my business was going great. I was signing up new clients, organizing things better, and being very productive in a lot less time. On most days I worked 9 AM to 4 PM. I handle 90% of the child-running-around chores, plus all the cooking. I spent a lot more time with the family, and I was making more money than I had ever made before.

That's when I started my Relax Focus Succeed® newsletter.

It occurred to me that everything I was doing could be duplicated by anyone – even without the pain and physical ailments.

So I went to work on figuring out why I had had such a dramatic boost in my personal and professional life. Was I just lucky? No, I wasn't willing to accept that. Was it just the meditation? The reading? The writing? No one element seemed to be the key.

Know Yourself

The first element might be self-knowledge. The more you know about yourself, the happier you'll be. Knowing yourself has other benefits as well.

Knowing your true self will help you work more effectively to reach your goals. It will lead you down the road to success. It will bring you a calmness that will improve your attitude and your relationships with others.

Psychologists spend most of their time trying to help people see things within themselves that they have been hiding from themselves. We humans are very adept at such games. If we don't want to deal with something, we deny that it happened, or we re-interpret it to fit a different view of the world.

I once had a startling conversation with my mother that revealed to me how completely we can fool ourselves.

> If you want to "know yourself" you need to take time to work at knowing yourself.

She casually mentioned doing something with my ex-wife and I asked when it happened. She said "when you came to visit from Michigan." I could not place what she was talking about. I had absolutely no recollection of a visit that had occurred a few years before.

"Isn't that interesting," she said. "You must not want to remember." She then gave me a picture taken at the time. Not only was it interesting, it was alarming. How could I simply forget a weeklong trip across the United States? The memory of my brief first marriage was powerfully painful. And what else have I "forgotten" or buried?

How easy it must be to ignore a comment or minor interchange. And what about things that were "remembered wrong" rather than forgotten altogether?

Humans have an amazing capacity to pay attention to just the things we want to. Have you ever watched non-kiddy television with a two-year-old in the room? Invariably, adults tune out the commercials and the kids tune out the TV show itself.

We do the same thing with newspapers and magazines. Some of us train ourselves to ignore the ads. We browse through the articles and ignore the ads. That's why advertisers are always doing something different to get our attention.

We pick and choose what we want to see. Our unconscious mind makes decisions about how to filter our experiences and sensory "input." And we're all different in what we filter and how we filter it. Have you ever heard someone say, "I never pay attention to . . ." something? One person might not know the color of her neighbor's car. Another might not know the major street names in his own neighborhood.

These are minor examples. But our minds use the same process to interpret every aspect of our personal and business lives as well. Was that tone in my wife's voice irritation or just fatigue? Does the boss expect me to work late or is that just my perception?

I once had a boss who stated very plainly that no one had to stay after 5 PM. He always did. And others always seemed to be around with him. Many of them believed it was part of their job to be there when he was there. Was this his intention or merely their perception?

We can take steps to make clear our intentions. I once had a client with more than a hundred employees who actually flashed the lights off and on at 5:10 PM. The message is clear: Go Home.

Sometimes we have to work hard to be understood. Some people have built tough, thick shells around themselves and it's impossible for you to break through. A person with extremely low self-esteem will see an accolade as a criticism.

"The boss thinks I'm such a loser that, when I finally do something right, she makes me employee of the month."

Well, there's very little you can do to change that person's negative perspective.

But what about yourself? How are *you* interpreting *your* world? What do you ignore in yourself and others? Many of us are just too busy to slow down and examine what we do and how we filter our world.

If you want to "know yourself" you need to take time to work at knowing yourself.

Who are you? What are your goals? Where do you want to be in five years? What do you want in your relationship with your spouse? How's your relationship with your children? What have you done to get to know your neighbors? What hobbies would you like to renew? What makes you happy? How often do you do things that make you happy?

What are you thankful for?

As with so many things in life, the road to happiness and success is easy, but we have made it more difficult than it needs to be.

When I ask you what makes you happy today, there are two possible answers. The first answer is superficial – it's the parlor game level of self-awareness. You might say money, or sex, or time to go on a date with your spouse. I'm not saying that this superficial answer is untrue, but it is probably trite. It doesn't have any personal meaning for you and the answer could be different tomorrow and the day after that.

The other answer you can give is a well-considered, principle-centered reflection of who you are and what you value. This statement does not have to be long and complicated. It

need not involve a lengthy discussion of the relative importance of competing values in your life. In fact, the "true"
answer to what makes you happy can be short and sweet.
For example, "My family makes me happy."

To others, this sounds like every other answer given around
the table. But your well-considered, "true" answer to the question will not change tomorrow or next week or next month. It
is also defensible. No matter how people might argue and ask
"what-if" questions, you can support your answer.

Parlor games aside, the process of knowing these types of
things about yourself takes a long time. You need to relax
and make yourself aware of who you are. And then the
answers will make themselves known to you.

So now I've made this process sound long and complicated.
But I've already made the claim that the process was to be
simple. It is simple. The process involves taking time every
day to sit and relax and think about yourself.

That's it. Simple.

You don't believe me, do you? You want the long, complicated answer that involves exercises you can do, lists to
make, inventories of your values, self-awareness questions,
long personal evaluation worksheets, mission statements,
and all that jazz.

You may want that because then you'll have every excuse to
not participate, or to quit after a few weeks.

Or you may want that because our society has told you that
successful people are dynamos, real go-getters. And we love
quick-fix solutions. Our collective closets are filled with

ten-minute-a-day exercise machines and our bookshelves are loaded down with advice on losing weight without trying and getting rich without working.

You have to work at anything you want. You want to get rich? Work at it. You want to be happy? Work at it. You want a good marriage? Work at it.

The process of getting to know yourself is very simple. Relax. Focus. Think.

I will tell you my "plan" – what I do to relax and focus and get to know myself. But my way is not the only way. Once you spend some time and begin to have some success you will think of things that work better for you.

It may take a month of relaxing and thinking before your method of relaxing and focusing reveals itself. Then you'll believe me. You'll say, "This is so simple. I could have figured this out if I had just sat down and relaxed and focused every day."

Alrighty then. Let's get started. I'm going to tell you what works for me. Feel free to make changes. Remember that the keys to success are:

- You must set aside time every day. Twenty minutes, thirty minutes. Maybe an hour on Saturday.

- You must relax. This takes practice because the hurry-up-and-be-successful person inside you doesn't want to relax.

- You must focus. Examining yourself is difficult. Not yourself as a parent or spouse or boss or worker or whatever. Yourself as you.

All of these things will be difficult at first. But they get easier over time.

The first twenty minutes you spend on this process will be difficult and not very productive. When you finally find twenty minutes to sit quietly your mind will not relax and you will experience a flood of thoughts about bills and family and work. You will not have much focus.

But don't worry. This is the inevitable process you have to go through. You will develop the habit of setting aside time. You will learn to relax. You will train yourself to focus. And then you will have a flood of energy, renewed vigor, and happiness in all aspects of your life.

I promise.

"The Unexamined Life is Not Worth Living"

I'm sure you've read this quote before: "The unexamined life is not worth living." Socrates said that at his trial for heresy. He was on trial for encouraging his students to challenge the accepted beliefs of the time and think for themselves. The sentence was death, but Socrates had the option of suggesting an alternative punishment. He could have chosen life in prison or exile, and would likely have avoided death.

But Socrates believed that these alternatives would rob him of the only thing that made life useful: Examining the world around him and discussing how to make the world a better place. Without his "examined life" there was no point in living. So he suggested that Athens reward him for his service to society. The result, of course, is that they had no alternative and were forced to vote for a punishment of death.

Luckily, we don't have to choose between an examined life and death. But the sad thing is, most people avoid leading an examined life. It's not that they don't have time or make time. They actively avoid examining their lives.

People who do examine their lives, who think about where they've been, how they got here, and where they're going,

> The hardest thing about examining your life is getting started.

are much happier people. No one has all the answers. And no one's life is free from trouble and strife. But those who have some sense of where they belong in the universe also have a context for understanding how all the elements of their life fit together.

If there are two people, one with a map and one without a map, who has the better chance of reaching her destination? The one with the map, of course.

When you set aside time to examine your life,

You get to choose your destination; You get to set the goals;

You get to determine the path; You get to decide how long it will take;

You get to decide whether you're on the right path or the wrong path.

In other words, you begin to know yourself and to take control of your life. You decide who you want to be and begin to become the person you want to be.

Examining your life brings tremendous freedom. You can take control of your life and all you have to do is set aside half an hour a day to get started. For specifics on getting started, go to http://www.relaxfocussucceed.com.

The hardest thing about examining your life is getting started. You have to sit your butt in a chair and get used to not doing anything. Just relax. Focus. Well, you understand . . ..

We Are All Many People

One of the themes you'll see throughout this book is my belief that we are all many people. Think about the people you've been: a child, a student, a graduate, a young person on your first job, a professional.

Perhaps you've been a married person, a manager, a business owner. Or you changed careers, went back to school, or took time off.

Look back five years and ten years and fifteen years: those are all different people than you are today.

It's too easy to say that people don't like change. People seek consistency and comfort. That's not a resistance to change. Humans have dreams and longings in their hearts. So while one part of them wants consistency, another part hungers for change.

Every disappointment in our lives, even a little one, reflects a desire for change. After all, if you're unhappy with the way things are, then whatever happiness is, it involves change from the way things are.

We evolve. We respond to our environment. Society gives us a path until we're about eighteen years old. Then, for the next five to ten years, we realize that no one's providing a plan anymore. We have to plot our own course.

> **Did you drift through the last five years?**

Many people – too many people – drift through their lives without a plan or a plot. They set one goal at a time and put little or no energy into it. It is my personal believe that midlife crises, as we call them, are just people waking up for the first time and asking "How did I get here? This is not the life I would have chosen for myself."

Sadly enough, they "got there" because the world keeps turning, life happens every day, and they allowed themselves to respond to their environment and never take an active role in choosing where they want to go.

This is doubly sad because the person with the midlife crisis is a lost soul AND very often ruins a marriage and a family in a sudden fit of needing to have a little control.

Too many people are human pinballs, bouncing around and reacting to life rather than taking control and doing something. You cannot be merely reactive to everything in your life for ten or twenty years and expect all your dreams to come true.

You have to take control of yourself and your dreams. You have to *have* dreams and you need to have a plan for making your dreams come true. No one else on earth has the job of making your dreams come true.

Let's assume that either 1) You aren't the person you want to be, or 2) You have dreams of a more fulfilling, relaxed, successful life. In either case, the path to success starts with you taking control of your life and deciding that you want to become a new person.

Once you have that decision in place, you can begin the hard work that really matters: Building your dreams and making them come true. Once you have a vision of the new you, then you can focus on it. The more you focus, the faster it will come true. It can't happen overnight, but it can happen a lot faster than you imagine.

Remember, focusing on your success is your super power!

NOTE: I think you should go through this in the order it is written. But if you're really jazzed about this topic, you can skip ahead and read Chapter Ten. But be sure to come back and take up right here again.

> No one else on earth has the job of making your dreams come true.

Working Toward Success is Like a Religion

You're about to undertake a very serious, fun, exciting, and difficult journey. For at least the first six months, your vision and goals may not be in good focus. But that's okay. You need to keep your focus on the *process* of being successful.

Putting your attention on being more successful will make you more successful.

Religions give us guidelines for how to live our lives. Sometimes the guidelines are very broad (e.g., Do unto others as you would have them do unto you) and sometimes they give very detailed and specific advice.

People fail. Even people who try very hard to practice their religion fail sometimes. Do you give up? Do you walk away? Of course not!

> Become the person you want to be. Gradually, slowly, and for the rest of your life.

The practice of your religion is not intended to make you perfect and then you never make any more mistakes. We're people – we're fallible. As weak, fallible humans, we practice religion in order to try to keep moving in the right direction. When we get "off track," religion helps us get back on track.

Working toward your success is the same way. You need guidance and direction and reminders about the path you're on.

If you make mistakes and become "less successful" or break one of the habits or rules you've set for yourself, don't worry. Get back on the path to success. Forgive yourself; learn from the experience; and set a plan to avoid this mistake in the future.

Success isn't a place you get to and stop. Success is a goal you strive for. It is a vision of excellence and accomplishment. It's a spectacular journey that never ends.

You will stumble and fall and fail. But that's not the end. Every day is a chance to start over, refocus your energy, and head in the right direction

The "Program" Is Not The Answer

Nobody has the answer. "The Answer" is found in the process of growing, evolving, improving yourself. It is tempting to get stuck on a program – to define yourself as part of a program.

Sometimes I get so "into" my program that I think my ideal schedule would be:

- One hour of meditation

- One hour of writing

- One hour of reading

- 30 minutes on the exercise bike

- 90 minutes of yoga

- and a long shower.

On some Saturdays I actually come close to this. You can see that, on a daily basis, this would really cut into your day.

According to my own exercises at focusing, the important things in my life are: My family; my personal development; and growing my business. There are several sub-goals for each of these areas. If I spend 4-5 hours a day working on a "program" that's supposed to help me improve myself, I would have a lot less time to live the things that are important to me.

Nowadays there are lots of 12-Step programs modeled after Alcoholics Anonymous. These are great programs that help millions of people, but every once in awhile someone gets "stuck" in the program.

If you haven't met someone like this yet, you will. Often they get stuck at the "I'm a person with a problem" stage and never get to the stages that help them improve their lives.

I see people who hate their jobs but don't quit. I believe it is possible for every one of us to find a job, or create a job, that we like so much that it is part of who we are. If you have a job that you love, then you don't dread going to work. And you don't long for retirement.

This is one example of bringing balance into your life. My wife works for the State and contemplates retiring one day. I don't anticipate retiring. As change is inevitable, I see that the mix of activities in my daily life will change over time. But I don't draw a big dark line between work and the rest of my life.

I love my work and I love my life. I know I'm blessed to have such a balance, but it didn't happen by accident. I worked on creating the balance and I work even today on maintaining the balance. I believe you can find balance too. If there's a "program," let it be one you create to bring into your life the balance that's right for you.

Don't get stuck on "the program." Don't define yourself as a person constantly working to find you who you are and what you want to do. Become the person you want to be. Gradually, slowly, and for the rest of your life.

Summary and Conclusions

Earlier in this chapter I said that I worked a long time trying to find the one thing that's the key to the "program" I developed for myself. I did eventually find it. And you may have guessed it.

Focus.

Focus like a laser beam.

But how do you know what to focus on? And how do you learn to focus?

First you relax. You take time to figure out who you are, what you want, where you want to go, how you want to get there, who you want to take with you, how fast you want to get there, and what you're willing to put up with along the way.

You may feel you've been tricked here. I've lumped all that thought process, introspection, meditation, reading, writing, and exercise into "Relax."

After you've figured all that out, then you can Focus.

Once you know what to focus on, then you can go to work.

And your Success is absolutely 100% guaranteed.

Relax

Focus

Succeed

How can I make such a bold claim? Read on!

To Ponder

"99% of the time, we know what we need to do to succeed–We're just unwilling to do it."

– Karl W. Palachuk

"Accessing wisdom requires little more than the confidence in knowing that when you quiet your mind, your mind isn't turned off."

– Richard Carlson

"One never finds life worth living. One always has to make it worth living."

– Harry Emerson Fosdick

Chapter 2

Working on Workaholism

Introduction

One of the great fallacies surrounding success is the belief that *hard work* and *more work* are the keys to success. There are three reasons why this belief is wrong.

The first reason working harder does not lead to success is that working *harder* and working *more* represent a violation of one of the basic laws of behavior:

> If you do more of the same,
> you'll get more of the same.

It's a natural reaction to work harder. After all, work is what we know. I put in eight hours, get a certain amount of work done, and I get paid a certain sum. So the natural calculation is: If I want more work done or more money, then it makes sense to put in more hours.

It's easy to fall into an extra hour here and an extra hour there. But gradually, over time, you find yourself working ten and twelve hours a day, then Saturdays and Sundays. Eventually you're just working all the time. But you're not making headway. Work seems to create work.

You're trapped and you feel like you're drowning.

And the main cause is that you went down the road of working more in order to get more done.

The second reason working harder does not lead to success is that putting in more hours is the lowest technical solution to any problem.

If you think about it, in a world without technology, your labor is all you have. But we do live in a world of technology. And we need to think about using technology to help us rather than just using more labor.

Using a unit of labor as a measurement of progress is very natural. Two easy examples are horsepower and manpower. Horsepower was originally based on the amount of pulling that could be accomplished by one horse. Of course today it's just a name given to a unit of *work done over time*.

A one horsepower motor can lift 33,000 pounds one foot in one minute. My generator has a one horsepower engine. But I don't need a horse. Technology has put that horsepower into a nice, convenient little package.

If I want a 300 horsepower engine, do I buy 300 horses? No. Technology has figured out a way to get the power from a piece of machinery.

But manpower is a different thing. When we calculate the jobs we have and the time they take, we can determine that our backlog is X person-hours. If I have 400 hours of backlog,

I can use 400 people working one hour each, or ten people working forty hours each.

Or I can work eighty hours a week and be done in five weeks.

Most of us don't even do that calculation. We just see a huge amount of work and we start working more and more. Most of us don't look to see how technology can improve this. We make no effort to find another process. We just work more or hire more people.

The third reason working harder does not lead to success is that working harder only improves progress for about four hours. Then everything begins to go downhill.

If you ever studied all night in college, you know there's a "point of diminishing returns." For most people, the best we can hope for is one eight hour day plus four more hours. After that, you're tired, irritable, you brain is stuck and you can't out-think the problem.

Every hour, every minute you spend on the problem is less productive. But some ancient instinct in our heads tells us that we're almost there. It makes us believe that progress is just around the corner.

If you do this once, you can recover quickly. But doing this two days in a row simply reduces productivity for the entire second day. And it gets worse on the third and fourth and fifth days.

In the meantime, you used to have a life. Boyfriend, girl-friend, spouse, cousin, friend, neighbor, dog. They're not getting the attention they deserve. And whether you like it or not, they're building a life that doesn't include you. Or it includes you a few hours a week. Then they're off doing their own thing.

I can't believe how many people have put off having a life until . . . sometime in the future. They don't really have a plan. Today they have to be successful. Why? Uh . . . because . . ..

They don't know where they're going, but they're working really hard to get there.

Two common milestones in life demonstrate this point. The first is retirement. People work hard all their lives, neglecting their families and even their own self as an individual. Then they retire and have no hobbies. Worse, their kids are gone and their spouses don't know how to spend more than three hours with them in the house.

The second example involves people who realize, in their forties, that they want a family. I saw a poster once of a woman looking very distressed. She was saying "Oh no. I forgot to get married."

This does happen to people. Work is such a central part of their lives that they really don't have anything else. No hobbies, no activities, no social life. After all, when you work ten to twelve hours a day, you're going to come home exhausted. You'll go to sleep and then get up and do it all again.

Days, weeks, months, and years fly by. Working, working, working.

The bottom line is that too much work means no balance in your life.

Too many people are working too hard – for nothing. They have no personal life, no goals, no plan. So they're burning themselves out and they don't even know why.

I'm not opposed to hard work. If you have goals and a plan, then I will support your hard work to achieve those goals. But if you don't know what you want, where you want to go, or how you want to get there, then that's what you should work on. Just a little effort on setting goals can focus your work in spectacular ways and bring meaning and fulfillment into your life.

This chapter covers a variety of ways to look at the work/life balance. Here we begin the important work of figuring out who you are and who you want to be, so you can determine the balance that works for you.

The Role of Inspiration

I think one of the most important contributors to your success is the ability to see qualities in other people that make you feel good and make you want to do better, work hard, and have the courage to try new things.

When I hear about a blind person climbing a mountain, I am inspired. When I hear about a young person doing something spectacular, I am inspired. When I hear about an old person who takes on great new challenges, I am inspired.

Most of us will find success by working hard every day, being persistent, and growing successful over time. But pointing to inspiring people and allowing ourselves to be impressed is very important. It teaches us that great things are possible. And great things are possible from normal people. That's good news, because most of us are normal!

And where do you find inspiration? That's the best part: it's everywhere! There are stories in the newspapers, magazines, and in all kinds of books. Even television occasionally moves away from "The Stupidest Contest We Could Think Of" and has inspiring stories.

> Do you allow yourself to be inspired? Or are you too cynical for that?

The key is, are you open to being inspired? Being open to inspiration is an attitude you take with you when you start your day. You have it when you stumble across a story, and you're able to receive the inspiration. If you carry cynicism and sarcasm throughout your day, then no feat will ever inspire you.

I recommend that you look for books with inspiring themes. These are often small collections of stories. When you have a minute or two, read a page or two. This habit will permanently improve your attitude. After all, if you start your day looking at the goodness and the greatness in the world, your predisposition will be toward the positive side of life. And that makes all the difference.

I have a little book entitled There's Always Time for Greatness: Who Did What When From Ages 1-100. A lot of it is simply "who did what," but there are some inspiring gems as well. Like Mozart giving concerts across Europe at age six, or Yehudi Menuhin playing violin solos with the San Francisco Symphony at age seven.

When we consider the outstanding feats of the young, it is humbling. There is a level of greatness I don't possess (and you can't go back to age seven). But impressive achievements should make us feel good about the human capacity to do great things.

I personally don't know how any human being can run a marathon. To me, that's impressive when anybody does it at any age. But I know it's *possible* and I know I could do it if I set my mind to it. I read that Dimitrion Yordanidis ran a marathon in Athens (in 7 hours, 33 minutes) at age 98! I cannot run a marathon today. And even if I start practicing, I won't be able to run one tomorrow. But sometime in the next fifty years? That I can do!

Sometimes, when we "grow up" we forget to dream. Maybe we get too busy. Maybe reality has too many pressing demands on us. Maybe we have to wait until the next raise, or the kids move out, or after the house is paid off. All of those excuses amount to one thing: Fear. Fear is a false barrier you put in front of yourself so you don't have to feel bad about not dreaming.

> Fear is a false barrier you put in front of yourself so you don't have to feel bad about not dreaming.

Inspiration can help you overcome fear (and drudgery, and boredom). Inspiration can bring you a life-giving force that allows you to dream. I think too many people stumble through life with a crippling view of what can be done. The truth is, anything can be done! First you have to be open to being inspired. Then come dreams and schemes. Eventually, actions have to follow because dreamers become dissatisfied with the here and now. Once you start considering *the possible*, you will want to move toward it – You will want to make it happen. It's a natural and extremely powerful series of events.

Begin today. Pick up one of the *Chicken Soup for the Soul* books. Or anything similar. Don't be so cynical. Goodness is everywhere when you take the time to look. So is greatness. And potential. And success. Begin by allowing yourself to be inspired.

Your Self vs. Yourselves

One reason psychologists and sociologists will always have plenty of work is that human beings are very complicated things.

We sometimes hear the admonition "Express Yourself." We ask children to paint and write and engage in other activities in order to help them express themselves. And we hope, in expressing themselves, the children will become themselves.

As we learn and grow, we try different things to see what we like. In some sense, we "try on" different personalities. The teen years are the most obvious example of this. In a perfect world, we would find the one single personality we like the best and keep it. Over time the personality we choose becomes who we "really" are. I'm going to refer to this as your *default personality*.

> You Are Who You
> Say You Are.
> So, Who Do You
> Say You Are?

But we never lose our free will, so we can always change who we are at any time. We just have to be aware that such changes can be very difficult.

When we find ourselves grown up and responsible, we also find ourselves operating in a variety of different settings. And with this we develop different personalities. For example, you might have the following personalities at some time or another:

Self

Spouse

Parent

Child (adult child)

Sibling

Professional

Community Member

and more.

Within some of these you might have additional personality sub-types. See Chapter Ten.

So far so good. This theory of personality roles is certainly nothing new or original. Literature from the earliest times until today addresses this subject. In fact, the literary technique of "putting on a mask" to play a different role is a mainstay of literature in all societies. Perhaps the most widely know examples are the play-within-a-play story lines of Shakespeare.

Personalities and Stress

Going through your day, week, and life balancing different personalities can be very stressful.

The greatest stress comes from situations in which the role you play is very different from the default personality you develop for yourself. Your default personality is the most comfortable one for you. So, the roles you play that are closest to your default personality are also the most comfortable for you.

In this diagram I show the default personality as "You" and the roles you play in relation to it. Some roles are closer, some further away.

For example, we often hear about the actor or politician who is really shy: Such a person puts on an outgoing personality when needed, but has a default personality that is much more shy.

You can see that this could be quite stressful.

There are three methods for addressing the problem of "space" between your default personality and the roles you play.

First, you can move the roles you play closer to your default personality.

Second, you can move your default personality closer to your roles.

Third, you can develop ways to accept the roles you play and find ways to accept the "space." This is the least satisfying route as the natural tension will always exist and you will always be working to reduce the stress.

Perhaps the lowest stress combination exists when the "you" at work and the "you" at home and all the other you's are all very similar. Thus you don't have the stress of putting on a mask and putting on a show.

But most of us have a great deal invested in our personalities. Bringing those personalities together and making them consistent takes a great deal of work. This is hard work, really, because it means we have to make changes to our default personality as well as all the other roles we play.

You Are Who You Say You Are.
So, Who Do You Say You Are?

This is where personal goal-setting and quiet time come in. Personal goal-setting starts with the basic question of who you want to be. When you look down the road five or ten years, how would you like to see yourself? Don't focus on how to get there! That comes later. Start by simply creating a vision of what you want to be.

Quiet time is the most powerful tool you have for reaching your goals. The benefits are two-fold. First, by sitting and giving yourself time to think about what you want, you begin to draw pictures of your future self. You make an outline and begin filling in the details. Second, the process of quietly thinking about where you want to go will result in moving in that direction. Even if you never create an elaborate step-by-step plan, having a vision of your future self will move you in that direction.

You will be a different person five years from now. Time will march on. Change will come whether you like it or not. The economy will ebb and flow. People will change, work will change, social settings will change.

It is up to you to choose: Will you simply float along for the next five years, with your default personality defined as a series of reactions to what's going on around you? Or will you choose who you will become and use the change all around you to move in that direction?

I hope you'll choose the second option. And begin today by spending a little quiet time working on it. See the meditation below.

> "Spiritual living is a fulfillment from moment to moment, in which the outer person is in a state of

living rapport with the inner being and becomes an extension thereof."

– N. Sri Ram

The Myth of Multi-Tasking

One of the big buzz words of the last ten years is "Multi-Tasking." I'm sure you've heard people say they're multi-tasking. Or perhaps you've prided yourself on being a multi-tasker. I've even seen people ask for this quality in formal job descriptions.

But there is no multi-tasking. People cannot multi-task.

We get this term from the world of computers. Despite the fact that we computer people have used this term for almost two decades, computers are just now being designed so they can do more than one task at a time. So, you see, even computers are not really multi-tasking.

A computer with one processor can only do one thing at a time. Computers have the wonderful facility of being very fast and being able to change tasks very quickly. So, when it looks like you are word processing and browsing the internet and editing a picture all at the same time, the computer is not really multi-tasking.

Computers operate by time slicing. Time slicing consists of giving a few milliseconds to one task, then a few to the next, then a few to the next. Because computers can change tasks so quickly, they appear to be doing two things at once. But in reality there is no multi-tasking.

You cannot multi-task either.

Sometimes we are engaged in several actions as the same time, but we cannot actually do them all at the same time. And, as humans are slow to change from one task to another, it is clearly visible that we have to stop doing one thing and start doing another.

No matter how quickly you switch tasks, you can never give your attention to two activities at the same time. You can *time-slice*. But your time slicing has limited effectiveness.

> If you try to multi-task you will divide your focus and the quality of your thinking will diminish.

The most important point for you to remember when you try to time-slice is that it reduces your overall effectiveness. We fool ourselves into believing that we are being more productive (or that other people are more productive) when we multi-task. In reality, you have split your attention between several tasks and therefore reduced your ability to focus on each task.

The more you focus on the task at hand, the more effective you will be. If you cloud your mind by trying to think about two or three things simultaneously, you will be less effective at each of them.

When writing a letter, for example, you should focus all of your attention on the letter. You will write faster, write more clearly, address the topic more effectively, and be done sooner than if you force your mind to switch back and forth between the letter and something else.

Sometimes we engage in a task but find it difficult. Writing is a good example. When the words don't come, we engage in something else. This is obviously the wrong thing to do. The words won't come until you give them your attention and focus on the writing. When you engage in something else, you make the writing less focused and less effective. The same is true for every other activity.

There are some activities that are particularly well suited for time slicing. Other activities can be organized around effective time slicing. Cooking is a great example of time slicing. You might put a roast in the oven and then, while it cooks, start preparing the vegetables. People who are very well organized and good at changing their focus can become great cooks and prepare seven courses with perfect timing.

I can barbeque hot dogs.

You can become efficient at time slicing. But never divide your focus.

You must develop the habit of discerning your most important task and focusing on that task until it is complete (or at a logical stopping point such as completing a draft that needs review). Then decide on your next most important task and focus all of your attention on that task until it is complete.

We have gone so far down the road of believing in multi-tasking that most of us have never developed the habit of focusing our attention on one thing at a time. Your job may require you to time-slice, but you must not think of it in those terms. Do not fool yourself into believing that you can do two things at once. The best you can do is to perform a poor job on two or three projects.

If you try to multi-task you will divide your focus and the quality of your thinking will diminish.

Begin today. Develop the habit of focusing all your attention on one thing at a time. You'll be amazed at how efficient you will become.

When you're excellent at focusing on one thing at a time, then you can begin training yourself to time-slice effectively that is, switching from one task to another. But once you switch, you must give all of your focus to the new task. If you try to think about two things at once or do two things at once, you will do neither of them well.

> You can become efficient at time slicing. But never divide your focus.

So-called Multi-Tasking is the root of many errors, poor workmanship, and stress. Do not ask yourself to do two things at once. And don't ask others to do it either.

Overcoming Workaholism

Have you ever heard the statement that "Americans are lazy"? That statement is patently absurd. Americans work their tails off. We work long hours. Sometimes two jobs. We hustle and bustle and squeeze in work during lunch.

The problem is, we're poorly focused. We're busy with busy work. We need to stop sometimes,

Focus every action on the goals,

set Priorities,

and make time to Relax

Focus

Exercise

Take time for family

Take time for a lunch break

Go home at 5 or 6

Less busy work and more balance.

Balance life and work.

Psychologists might disagree, but I've always thought that the human mind is like a file drawer that wants to be organized. We access pieces of our brain all day information we have and old memories in order to build new thoughts.

All day long we take files out of the drawer. Problems and "new things" that come up have to be put into the drawer, along with all that stuff we took out.

"The Secret of Success is Consistency of Purpose."
– Benjamin Disraeli

Rest, relaxation, contemplative thought: These are the tools we use to organize the drawer.

We lead lives filled with deadlines and too much work, and chaos, and bills, and we're always on the go-go-go. We don't stop, look around, and change directions. We just go where the work and the kids and the world take us.

Our "schedules" are full of things, full of details. Most of those things have been put on our schedule by someone else, or by necessity. So we're busy-busy-busy with the everyday chores and we don't focus on the longer-term goals. Every once in awhile we need to poke our heads up above the cubicle maze and see whether we're getting closer to where we want to be.

> We all know that slowing down a little and doing it right will save work in the long run.

Many of us are trapped in the maze because we're on the "easy road to success." The easy road to success is a lie we tell ourselves. I don't know why.

The Indispensible You

We see clearly in others what we do not see in ourselves. For example, my wife always knows when I need to go to the doctor, but never thinks she needs to go. "Oh that punctured lung? It's just a rib out of place. There's nothing the doctor can do anyway."

This is especially true with workaholism. My pile of work *will never get done* and must have my attention. Someone else's pile of work *will never get done* and he should realize that.

I used to think the work couldn't get done without me. I think that's the biggest pitfall for most of us.

We take on a job and discover that there's too much work for a 40-hour week. The boss seems to work 50 or 60 or 70 hours. So we work through lunch and come in early and stay late. Then we go in on the weekend. We work more and more and more.

We fool ourselves four ways with this behavior:

1. We tell ourselves this is short-term. Once we get the work caught up, we'll go back to 40 hours.

2. We tell ourselves that we're indispensable. No one else can do this. Oh, sure, you can train people, but they won't be as diligent and you don't have the time. Some knowledge you just can't pass on.

3. We tell ourselves (or maybe we've been told by others) that there's a big reward at the end of the year (or end of the project). So we're working for the bonus. But then what? Aren't you going to want the next bonus too?

4. We tell ourselves that we're doing this for the family. This is for the long-term benefit of the spouse and kids. But spouse and kids have to feel alive too.

We fool ourselves because we want to fool ourselves.

We're intoxicated by work. I believe men are more susceptible to this than women. But anyone who is raised to measure success in terms of "work," and who defines himself by what he does "for a living" is a potential workaholic.

And our culture reinforces this perspective. At a party you meet someone. The first question is "What do you do?" If you answer "I'm a father of two and I collect fountain pens" there will be a long silence. "Okaaaaaay" they'll say, "and what do you do for a living?" Try this at your next party. It's fun.

It's as if we can't discuss the non-work "you" until we get the work conversation out of the way.

After a long process of distilling my life and focusing my energies on where I want to go, I have developed the habit of defining for myself three goals every morning. I write down the following three things every day:

- What's the most important thing I want to do today for myself personally?

- What's the most important thing I want to do today for my family?

- What's the most important thing I want to do today for my work?

(Note: Sometimes I add a fourth category – community. The first three categories are the most important, and the most universal. We all need to take care of ourselves, our families, and our work. On the next tier of important things to take care of we find "community." This includes your neighborhood, your church, business communities, etc.

Sometimes I will refer to three categories. That will always be the three primary categories listed above. When I mention four categories, that will include community as well.)

More details later.

The point here is that I have defined the three pieces of my life that make up almost all of who I am. Work is extremely important. It is silly to think otherwise. But work has its place and must fit comfortably in the big plan with Personal Self and Family Self.

Every workaholic will eventually have an experience that shatters the imaginary world we've built. We don't see it coming because we've fooled ourselves.

The event that slaps you in the face with reality might be dramatic or simple. You might get laid off. Or passed over for a promotion in favor of a clock-watcher who never comes in on the weekends. You might take off a week for vacation and discover that the business was fine without you.

For me the eye-opener was a disagreement over a bonus. I had completely fooled myself into believing that my hard work, extra hours, and neglecting my family would be justly rewarded. I took on extra work and made major contributions to the company in several areas. I traveled all over the U.S. for a year, negotiated a major contract, set up a new office in another state, oversaw the newest product development for the company, and much more.

I worked myself to the point of exhaustion and hit homeruns all year.

And when it came time to review my annual performance I got 80% of my potential bonus for the year. I was devastated. As a former teacher I view 80% as a B-minus. I know my performance wasn't perfect and I'd hung up the phone on a company lawyer once but certainly I deserved something in the "A" range for all my successes.

In an instant my eyes were opened. Before I'd blinked twice my life had changed. For the price of a few hundred dollars the company could have bought a repeat performance for the next year. But it wasn't worth it to them.

Before I spoke a word, I knew that I would put in 40-hour weeks from that point forward. I knew I would leave my desk at lunch. I knew I would use up my vacation time. I knew I would find another job.

What I didn't know at the time is that my boss had already decided to leave the company. She wanted to keep expenses down in order to maximize her bonus. She didn't care about the future profitability of the company. And she didn't care about my personal loyalty to her.

I had fooled myself into working like a madman in search of a reward that was only a pittance.

I guess I was lucky to learn this lesson over a bonus rather than over a firing. My experience changed my attitude toward work forever. Not that I became a clock-watcher, but now I try to have realistic expectations about how valuable I am to "the company."

When I took my next job, I had a very open and honest discussion about what they expected from me. They outlined a week that looked like 40-50 hours. I agreed to that. And because we had this discussion before I started, I never felt any pressure to work longer hours.

Sometimes our lives evolve and we don't realize what's going on until years later. I am now a computer consultant. I still work 40-50 hour weeks. I joke with my clients that I work half days and I get to pick the 12 hours. I now have lots of bosses: my clients. And I have lots of work because there are clear understandings between my clients and me.

They agree to pay a specific price for specific work. I offer up so many hours at a certain rate. No one expects to get a bunch of hours for free. If I work hours for free, it's my choice. No bonuses, and I know that.

Because expectations over hours and pay were a major issue for me awhile back, it is natural that I would evolve to create a job in which this relationship is very clear.

I still have to fight my workaholic tendencies. But the issues of pay and hours are now very low-stress for me.

Slow Down: Get More Done

One of my great weaknesses is that I want to jump into a job, get it done, and move on. Sort of a "surgical strike" to solving computer problems. This is a weakness because it can lead to neglecting the people side of the business. It also means I have a tendency to be focused on the next job instead of the present job.

As part of my business ethic, I am very attentive to clients' computer needs. Rather than just fix the problem at hand, I take a minute and apply software updates and make sure "automatic" maintenance is running.

But I don't always take time to say "Hello. How are you?" and make the personal contact.

Having employees has helped me on this score. As I train them, I put a lot of emphasis on focusing on the present job rather than worrying about the next job. I've developed a formula for a customer visit – the KPEnterprises way of performing an office visit.

The goal is to provide a consistent, positive experience for the customer. And for me it means I end up preaching about the one thing I need to focus on. Take time – a few minutes – and chat with the customer. This builds a personal relationship, it keeps the atmosphere relaxed, and it makes the job enjoyable.

I tell prospective employees that one of the benefits to working for me is that you get to work with nice people. I cultivate clients who are enjoyable to be around. But, truth be told, 99% of the population are nice people if you stop and take a minute to talk with them.

Taking your time also means relaxing when you have to do all those little things we often consider "necessary" distractions from our "real" job. This includes filing papers, balancing the checkbook, driving between appointments, reading reports, employee evaluations – any little thing you tend to rush through.

Take your time. Relax. Do it right. Focus on the current job. When you've finished you can move on to the next job.

Our society and our work culture tend to emphasize working fast – often faster than it really takes to get the job done. Sometimes we find ourselves with too few people and too much work. The go-go-go mentality results in sloppy work, incomplete work, and no time to focus on quality.

I once worked at a place like this. The manager sometimes joked "We never have time to do it right but we always have time to do it over." We all know (if we take time to think about it) that slowing down a little and doing it right will save work in the long run. Relaxing a bit can also save a lot of stress.

A great example of this is in the car. Did you ever notice one of those people who passes you at 20 miles over the speed limit and you catch up with him at the next light? Then he takes off fast and zooms ahead, but you catch up with him at the next light. After a few miles this gets to be pretty funny. One of you is more stressed than the other.

And even if Mr. Stress gets ahead of you by a light, he may only save three minutes in his cross-town travel!

Slow down. Relax. Focus on the task at hand. Do it right. You'll produce a higher quality product and you won't have to do it over.

Take your time and you have more time.

Take Advice!

Take my advice: Take other people's advice.

The bookshelves at the library are filled with books on success. Whether you want to find seven secrets of success, think and grow rich, stop sweating the little things, or learn to put first things first: There's a world of great advice out there.

In addition, you know lots of successful people. Think about it and look around. In your work, through your neighbors, and at the local stores you visit, the world is full of people who are working hard and doing well.

As you talk to these people – and read these books – you'll find an abundance of great advice.

Take it.

As humans, we seem always to be seeking advice. But for some reason we resist taking the advice we seek! The first time I read *The Greatest Secret in the World*, I was struck with Og Mandino's attitude. He starts out by saying that most people who start the book won't finish it and most people won't take the advice and do the exercises. Almost no one will take his advice.

And he's right. He's also correct that those who do take his advice will be more successful than those who don't. So why not take his advice?

> Anytime that you decide to focus and spend a year of your life becoming successful, you will be successful.

What's up with us, as humans, that we can't take advice we know we should take?

I can't summarize all the good advice in the world, but I can give some examples.

If you read ten pages a day of some book on success, that's 3650 pages a year. That's a lot of books. I hope this is the absolute minimum you are willing to commit to your own success and happiness. It's equivalent to at least ten books a year.

[**Stop:** You've just been given advice. Will you do it?]

And in these ten books you are very likely to come across each of the following pieces of advice in at least six of the books:

> Exercise at least three or four times a week.

> Take time regularly to focus on your goals.

> Write down your goals.

> Read books on anything and apply it to your success.

> Do something to reduce stress regularly (quiet time, meditation, relaxation exercise, etc.)

> Write down your values and your "mission statement."

> Develop a process for planning your day, your week, your month, your year.

> Do something every day to focus on success – even for a few minutes.

You will read all kinds of variations on these themes. You will see them again and again and again.

You will be told many times that daily relaxation exercises and focusing on success are the keys to happiness, balance, and wealth. There should be no doubt in your mind that the road to your success is a variation on these themes.

Will

You

Do

It?

Most people accept intellectually that they need to do these things. But for some reason only a few people ever take this advice.

I don't know why. Perhaps we've all worked so hard to get where we are that we don't have the energy to "start over" with a program that requires work and attention and focus.

At a minimum, please keep up the reading. If you read the advice enough times, perhaps you'll try one thing. And then another.

The great news is that its never too late. Anytime that you decide to focus and spend a year of your life becoming successful, you will be successful.

So please do at least one thing for yourself: get in the habit of reading books on success. Someday when you have time to actually become successful you can take the rest of the advice.

Summary and Conclusions

Let's be honest: workaholics run the world.

They also have more than their share of heart attacks, strokes, cancer, and a variety of other ailments. That's because they also have more than their share of stress.

Workaholics also spend a lot of time and energy in the very unproductive hours after they've already put in a ten hour day.

On one hand, they get credit for working 14 hours a day. On the other hand, many of these hours are worked at 50%, or 40%, or 20% effectiveness. They spin their wheels faster and faster but don't get very far.

If you're in this situation, you will eventually come to realize that it only leads to more fruitless hard work. You can learn that from experience. Or you can learn it from taking someone's advice.

You get to decide.

Just beware. If you think the rules don't apply to you, or that you can work harder and faster and never burn out, you have a much harder lesson to learn than those who learn from taking advice.

In the next chapter we'll start the hard work that really matters.

To Ponder

"One's action ought to come out of an achieved stillness: not to be a mere rushing on."
                        – D.H. Lawrence

"Success that brings only stress and chases away relationships is not really success at all."
                        – Karl W. Palachuk

"What does it matter how much we do if what we're doing isn't what matters most?"
                        – Stephen R. Covey

Chapter 3

Habits, Knowledge, and Tools

Introduction

Now that you have an understanding of the basic philosophy of Relax Focus Succeed®, we're going to look at some of the tools and attitudes of success.

Everything you do requires the right "tools" and the right skills. If you're cooking, you need pots and pans, and the skill to turn ingredients into a meal. The same is true for writing contracts, plumbing, fixing a car, setting up a swing set, and every other activity in your life.

Working on success is no different. You need the tools of success.

Exactly what do you need to be successful? Let's make a list:

- Determination
- Knowledge
- Talent / Skill

- Experience
- Intelligence
- Genius
- Perseverance
- Money
- The Right tools
- Focus

And you may add some other elements.

> What some people call genius may just be hard work!

If you put these into categories you'll see that they are all habits, knowledge, or tools.

Habits can be acquired. You have to decide that you want to work for something. Then you decide what you need to do in order to achieve that something. Then you develop the habits that will get you there. This includes determination, perseverance, and focus.

Knowledge, which includes talent, intelligence, and even "genius" can be acquired. The two most obvious methods are experience and reading. Remember the words of Thomas Edison: "Genius is two percent inspiration and ninety-eight percent perspiration." What some people call genius may just be hard work!

Tools include money and equipment. You acquire these with time. And perseverance, and skill, and hard work, all of which are in your grasp!

In this chapter, we'll look at some of the habits, knowledge, and tools you need to be successful. We'll look at attitudes and habits most closely.

> Habits.
> Knowledge.
> Tools.

The Fred Flintstone-Ralph Cramden School Of Success

Success is an odd thing. Almost everyone knows how to be successful but almost no one chooses to work at it. How can you be successful? You get up every day, work hard, practice your trade, improve yourself, set goals, and work toward them.

Some people think they will stumble onto wealth. This is the Fred Flintstone-Ralph Cramden School of Success. There's always a scheme. They take money from their retirement fund and stick it into a pet rock franchise. Or they invest in a real business but don't show up to work. In the Fred Flintstone-Ralph Cramden School of Success there is no hard work. There's only one fruitless scheme after another.

But that's not why most people don't succeed. It is related, however. Most people choose not to succeed because it's difficult. Success is much more than money. It means good personal relationships, happiness, financial security, and a well-rounded life filled with people and things that make you happy. Fred and Ralph never get any money, but supposedly learn that friends and family are what really matter. Of course they forget this in time for the next episode.

We all fail. We fail to exercise, even though we know we should. We fail to put away money for retirement. We fail to relax. We fail to continue improving our skills. We fail to dream.

> Most people choose not to succeed because it's difficult.

The great thing about success is that you can start over any time, any day. You can begin exercising today, and setting goals, and making time to relax, and getting to know yourself at a more meaningful level.

When you look back on the list of things you need to do for success, you'll see that most people do most of these things: they work hard, practice their trade, improve themselves. The one they don't do is to set goals. And that's the killer. If you don't set goals then all the hard work is useless.

Oddly enough, people are willing to work 50-60 hour weeks, take night classes, stick away some money for retirement, and yet have no idea why they're doing any of it!

Perhaps the single thing that separates successful people from everyone else is the willingness to think about their lives, get to know themselves, set goals for themselves, and work toward the goals. Rather than being mice on a treadmill, they step off the treadmill and consider where they've been, where they want to go, and how to get there.

So, why don't people do this? I have to admit I don't know. I think many people are caught up in the belief that they don't have the time. The work keeps piling up, the store has to be opened, the paperwork keeps flowing, and they don't have time to stop. The result is, they climb on the treadmill every day and run faster to go nowhere. They don't see that they're running faster and faster and faster with nowhere to go.

I've been in the position of needing to train someone but not having the time to do it. The result, of course, is that I keep doing the work until I take the time to train someone. Then, of course, I have more time because someone else is doing part of the work. I know what needs to be done, but I put it off because I perceived that I didn't have the time.

Success is the same way. Once you take the time to relax, think about your goals, and decide where you want to go, then all of your work is more meaningful. Your life is more meaningful! But you have to take the time to do it.

Resolve today. Step off the treadmill.

Lessons From Losing

Our society – and as far as I know every other society – places value on winning. This is good. Or, perhaps as a human living in a society, I have no option but to believe that this is good.

Winning brings out great qualities in people. It helps us to conquer our fears and ourselves. It helps us learn to work together, to set goals, and to measure our progress. The search for "winning" also has its dark side. The worst, perhaps, is what we do to our children in youth sports leagues: coaches telling seven-year-olds how to body slam and avoid a foul; parents calling their children "losers"; and so-called grown-ups fighting and screaming, and sometimes killing each other, over a game that just doesn't matter.

But this section is not about winning. I merely take as my premise that winning is good and learning to be a good winner is important.

> Maintaining focus and being totally aware of the moment at the time of loss will help you learn the most.

This section is about the value of *losing*. Losing has value precisely because winning has value. In all great endeavors – in all great victories and accomplishments – there is a lot of losing.

Remember the great story of Thomas Edison. He had the basic idea for the light bulb (the incandescent lamp) but had to work hard to find the right filament, bulb, base, and so forth. In his first hundred attempts the bulb either did not work or only worked for a very short while.

Edison was not discouraged by this (or at least he did not let on that he was discouraged). From his perspective, he had discovered a hundred ways *not* to make a light bulb.

When we learn to do anything, we first learn how not to do it. One of the blessings of being a parent is helping a child through the frustration of learning to walk, read, ride a bike, and a million other victories.

Sometimes we forget the frustrations we've been through. For example, we forget – either intentionally or unintentionally – the frustration of learning to ride a bike. But as we help a child, we come face to face with this frustration. And we want, as parents, to make it easy and to help the child learn. But we can only help so much.

At some point the child has to just keep trying until the bike stays upright. And suddenly, after trying hundreds of ways *not* to ride a bike, success is achieved. And instantly one more person begins to forget the frustration it took to learn to ride a bike.

When I think of all the things I've learned to do, I have to be honest and remember all the trials, tribulations, and mistakes along the way.

A great part of "winning" the human race is to focus on the good and the glorious and the victorious. But we grow better and we grow faster when we learn from our mistakes and our losses.

The Zen of Losing

Sometimes, when we stop to think about it, we find that we place value in winning even in the smallest, pettiest, most meaningless elements of our lives.

I once had a friend who cheated at Yahtzee. She always kept her score card close to her and always managed to get a bonus for the top of the score card. This was the first time in my life that I remember knowing that I could win or lose by simply doing something the other person couldn't stop. I could ask to keep score, I could check the scoring with each turn, or I could simply discuss the score and watch her write it down.

Instead I simply let things continue and paid attention to the patterns: when did she cheat, what did she say, how much pride did she take in winning this way?

I don't know how many thousands of games of Yahtzee I've played in my life. And when I'm dead and gone I don't think any one game will have meant much to me at all. So, I found myself playing and losing and not caring that I lost most of the time. And I found that I enjoyed playing just as much when winning and losing were removed from the equation.

My new approach to the game allowed me to view each game as if I were a third-party observer. I never felt the desperate need to win; I never made a rash decision; and I was able to "slow down" and view the patterns within the game.

Knowing that there were an endless number of games ahead, and winning was not an issue, I was able to try various approaches and compare their results. I tried different strategies and observed the lowest scores one could expect, how to maximize points on the bottom of the score card, and the best strategies for each of the three (yes, three) types of patterns in the game.

I also learned how to watch my opponent and see her reaction to the ebbs and flows of the game. When did she take risks and when did she play it safe? How did her demeanor change when she cheated?

Over time I became a better player. I learned strategies to increase my score for the part of the game I could control.

I also learned (for Yahtzee and other games):

- How to observe my opponent.

- How to "slow down" and remove myself from the action. Thus I see the whole game and my place in it.

- How to observe the parts of the game I control and those I cannot.

I learned to have a certain perspective about games and winning and losing generally. We tend to fall into a belief that we need to win in every situation. We need to win every stupid argument, every little game, every little thing.

A great example of our bizarre universal need to win is in our cars. Some people race from stop light to stop light. Those of us who don't do this "win" because we're superior to those who do. We refuse to let people in front of us when a lane disappears. Or we ride in that disappearing lane until it merges with the shoulder and we force our way into the already-merged traffic.

Another great experience for learning the Zen of losing is to have a child (or work with children). We all understand that children need to learn to win and to lose. Sometimes you'll see games for little kids in which no one wins and no one loses. After age two these games are fundamentally uninteresting to children.

Lesson One: Winning and losing does matter.

Children learn very quickly that winning is the goal. Children go through a stage in which they don't want to play unless they win. Of course you can't let them win all the time or they don't learn the important skill of losing. Admit it: You learn more sportsmanship from losing than from winning!

The value of losing only comes when you examine your loss. What did you do or not do? How did you act? Did you take the initiative or react to someone else? Were you focused on the job at hand?

Again, sports and games help us learn to lose as well as to win.

In the Olympics I am constantly amazed at some of the things human beings can do with their bodies. And I marvel at the tremendous heartbreak that must happen daily. How many times have we seen this story: An internationally recognized athlete performs "perfectly" in the trials. Then, in the final run she performs a personal best. She sets a national record, an Olympic record, and a world record. She's in first place and the gold medal is almost hers. She has done every single thing she can do to be the best. Then, a half hour later, someone does better. And now she's second place.

This is tremendous heartbreak. And yet we see it several times at each Olympics.

Lesson Two: Sometimes you can do everything right and still not win.

You can be trained and skilled, experienced, focused, prepared, have all the resources, know all the right people, make no mistakes – and still not win. You hang your head and say "Okay, remind me again about the value of losing."

Losing is inevitable. Everyone loses sometimes. That doesn't mean you give into it. That doesn't mean you accept it. Losing is simply a thing. It exists. It happens.

But losing is not who you are. Everyone loses. Even the winners. You're not a loser, you're a winner. The fact that you lose sometimes does not change the fact that you're a winner.

Learn from your losses. Be composed. Maintain your self control. Maintain focus.

Reflection helps, but maintaining focus and being totally aware of the moment at the time of loss will help you learn the most. Harsh, negative reactions will only get in the way.

The biggest winners are those who go right back into the game. Sales people who work for months on a sale and lose it are still winners when they show up for work the next day and go at it again.

So keep your perspective. Go to the gym and wear yourself out. Take the rest of the day off, and come back tomorrow a winner!

What to Read for Inspiration

Here's a million dollars worth of advice: Read.

Read anything and everything. Read morning, noon, and night. Reading will bring you success. If you've got some goals and some direction, then anything you read will help with your success.

Many people wonder, "What should I read to help me be successful?" My answer is "everything."

In a great little pamphlet on censorship entitled *Aeropogitica*, John Milton says that "A wise man will make better use of an idle pamphlet than a fool will do of sacred Scripture." In other words, if you (the reader) put your skill and reasoning into your reading, then you will find value in anything you read.

One of the interesting things about success and motivation is that, once you put your mind to something, you begin to see that thing more clearly. Once you are determined to find opportunities in a certain area, you begin to see those opportunities all the time. It's like when you buy a new car and suddenly begin to notice that kind of car all over the place. I never realized how many Accords there were until I started driving one. I never realized how many sales opportunities there were until I started looking for them.

This is known as focusing on opportunity. Once you begin to focus on opportunity, you will find it everywhere. The same is true for focusing on knowledge. Once you go through the process of setting goals and focusing your life on the personal and professional things that matter, you will find useful tips and tricks in everything you read!

> A wise man will make better use of an idle pamphlet than a fool will do of sacred Scripture.
> – John Milton

When I get ready to do something, I'll pick up a book and educate myself. Very often I find a book that motivates me in other areas of my life. For example, I've read books on managing rental property and buying commercial real estate that are very motivating generally. Believe it or not, even a technical exam preparation book can be motivating. When the author provides information and a can-do attitude, the reader finds himself saying "Yeah, I can do this. It's only a test."

Because of my areas of interest, I will see different information in a magazine than you will. Once you have areas of focus, you will find gems of information everywhere you look. For example:

> Fiction (historical or not) usually has a lot of good background information on whatever topic or setting makes the story go.

> Biographies are usually quite inspiring because the process of researching them usually causes the author to fall in love with the subject. And most biographies are about someone who contributed something to the world.

> Magazines are full of every kind of useful information. And sometimes they're not on the topic you suspect. Magazines need to keep pumping out information every month, so there's always some new perspective.

> Trade Books (that is, the technical side of your business) have useful information about your specific business. But most also have a theoretical or philosophical approach, or a section on "best practices."

> Hobby Books are great for the relaxation side of the equation. But they also have lessons on the basics of success: You can do this. Focus.

Take your time. Practice. You'll get better with experience. Etc.

Self-Help books are obviously useful. Be sure to be open to books that don't seem appealing at first. Remember, the important part of growth is to grow in the areas where you feel the least comfortable.

How-To Guides are a category that aren't really trade books and aren't really hobby books. You want to come up to speed on plumbing, creating a corporation, or designing a deck? There's a book for it! Because these books are written by people who love what they do, they are filled with a positive attitude and a sense that you're going to enjoy doing your new skill.

> Reading improves your vocabulary Inexorably!

The bottom line is obvious: Read. Everything.

Start today. There's no reason not to.

A Tale of Perseverance

There are many people who achieve truly grand goals by overcoming challenges and working at it a little every day.

Once upon a time there was a beetle who lived near the Pacific Ocean with his family. One day he took a nap on a leaf high in a tree. The wind began to blow and the tree shook. When the beetle awoke, the tree was swinging wildly. All at once, the leaf broke off from the tree and the beetle hung on for dear life as the leaf carried him up and up and far away.

The wind drove him in circles and then high in the air. Around and around. Up and down. Hour after hour. Until, finally, he came to rest in a desert.

The beetle looked around. He didn't know where he was. Soon, a scorpion wandered by. "Excuse me" said the beetle, "can you tell me where we are?"

The scorpion looked puzzled. "We are here" she said.

"Thank you," said the beetle, "but I am not from here. I live by the ocean. Can you tell me how to get back to the ocean?"

"The ocean is not here" said the scorpion. "The ocean is a long way off. You cannot get there."

The beetle was alarmed. "Why can't I get there?"

"Because," said the patient scorpion, "You are here and the ocean is a long way off. You can't walk that far."

The beetle was sad. "But I got here from far away. So I must be able to get back," he said.

"How did you get here?" asked the scorpion.

"I flew on this leaf" said the beetle.

"I don't know about flying," said the scorpion. "I only walk. And I know you can't walk to the ocean. Ask a bird about flying."

"Thank you," said the beetle.

Then the beetle looked around for a bird. He saw birds flying about, but none close enough to talk to. But in watching the birds he observed that they could fly easily in one direction but had great difficulty in the other. And as the sun set, the beetle settled down under his leaf to sleep. He noted that the sun sets in the direction the wind comes from. So, he concluded, the ocean must be there.

The next day the beetle rolled up his leaf and headed in the direction of the ocean. He walked all day, stopping occasionally to eat. After awhile a dragonfly came by. "Hello said the beetle.

"Hello" said the dragonfly. "Where are you going?"

"I'm going to the ocean," said the beetle.

"You can't get there" said the dragonfly. I am from the ocean. I know.

"Why can't I get there?" asked the beetle, alarmed once again.

"Because," said the dragonfly, "the wind almost always blows away from the ocean. You can't fly against the wind."

"So you go wherever the wind takes you?" asked the beetle.

"Of course," said the dragonfly. "What else can I do?"

"You can walk against the wind," said the beetle.

"No," said the dragonfly. It is a hundred miles to the ocean. Flying is much faster than walking. And when you fly, the wind almost always takes you away from the ocean.

"So you fly," said the beetle, "because it's faster than walking. But you don't fly where you want; you fly where the wind takes you."

"Yes, of course," replied the dragonfly. "Walking would be much too slow." With that, a breeze picked up and the dragonfly was off.

"Thank you," called the beetle. Then he began walking in the ocean direction, thinking about the dragonfly. "If the wind almost always blows away from the ocean, it must sometimes blow toward the ocean," he thought. "I will be prepared. When the wind blows toward the ocean, I will fly with my leaf. And when it does not blow toward the ocean, I will walk."

The beetle walked many days and many nights. When the wind flew toward the ocean he tried to fly on his leaf. It took him a long time to learn to fly the leaf. He tried many things that did not work until he eventually learned to control it. Sometimes the wind tricked him and he flew farther from the ocean.

But our friend was a very determined beetle. Despite the discouragement of flying poorly or flying in the wrong direction, he was dedicated to his goal. Whenever he landed, he took his bearings and began walking toward the ocean.

Then one day the beetle came to a large body of water. He found a slug and asked "Is this the ocean?"

"No," said the slug. "The ocean is a long way off. You can't get there from here."

"Why not?" asked the beetle.

"Because the ocean is on the other side of the lake," said the slug.

"How do I get to the other side?" asked the beetle.

The slug looked confused. "You don't" she said. "There is this side and there is the other side. You are on this side."

"Have you been to the other side?" inquired the beetle.

"No," replied the slug. "I am on this side."

"Do you like this side?" the beetle asked. "Is this side better than the other side?"

"This side is fine," said the slug. "I don't know about the other side. I know this side is fine."

"Can I walk around the lake?" asked the beetle.

"No," said the slug. "It would take too long."

"Too long for what?" asked the beetle.

"Well," replied the slug, "you don't want to go all the way over there and decide you like it better here. Then you'd just have to come back." And with that, she moved off to find some leaves to eat.

The beetle thought about his journey so far. He didn't seem to be making much progress. Everyone he met thought he was odd for wanting to make the journey. The scorpion could not imagine going anywhere. The dragonfly went fast but couldn't go where he wanted. He just went fast. The slug knew how to get around, but was afraid her effort would be wasted.

Were they all right? Was he foolish? He sat for a long time and thought about his plight. Finally, he decided that the others were foolish and not him. They had no purpose, or they floated aimlessly through life.

He knew what he wanted. He had devised clever ways to use the elements for his benefit. True, there were days when he went backwards and there were days spent making up time. But he knew he must be getting closer.

And so the beetle determined once again to find his way home. He rolled up his leaf and headed around the lake. Eventually the beetle made his way around the lake and gradually got closer and closer to the ocean. Then one day he caught sight of a large rock formation he recognized. Right away he knew he would be successful.

On the last few days of his journey the beetle thought about his success. "I am successful because I persevere," he said. And he went on:

- "I am successful because I know that I don't know everything."

- "I am successful because I am willing to try things I haven't done before – even if I'm scared."

- "I am successful because I don't give up when I have discouraging days or big setbacks."

- "I am successful because I take time to focus on my goals and remind myself where I'm going."

- "I am successful because I know I don't have to make a great progress every day."

- "And I learned that I don't have to think about the big 'impossible' goal all the time. Every day I work to accomplish the simple little work that moves me toward the bigger goal."

End of the Tale

Summary and Conclusions

When people achieve great things we often analyze them. Two classic examples are centurions and sports figures. Reporters always feel obligated to ask people what they did to live the age of 100 years. The answers are often cute and seldom informative. "I got up every day and I didn't die that day, so I got up the next day. Before I knew it I was 100."

Sports figures tend to give better answers. This is especially true of goals that are grandiose. The most points ever scored in a lifetime. Ten years without missing a game. Best in the league five years in a row.

When asked about these milestones, athletes tend to say something like "I didn't start out with this goal. I just went to work every day, worked hard, and earned my pay. When I realized this record was reachable, I started focusing on it. I thought a little about it every day. But there's nothing you can do all at once. You have to go to work every day, work hard, and earn your pay."

The same thing happens a million times a year with less-publicized goals. Ordinary people walk across America, climb Half Dome, complete marathons, graduate from college, pay off their mortgage, celebrate five years of sobriety, or celebrate 50 years of marriage.

These are awesome goals and we should not minimize them. And yet all these miraculous achievements stem from normal daily living. You can't get married one day and celebrate 20 or 40 or 50 years the next day. You have to get up every day, be a married person, work on it (and don't die), then get up the next day and be a married person some more.

Miraculous events sometimes grow out of simple hobbies. I have a friend who has juvenile-onsite diabetes. He has to constantly monitor his body and keep a delicate balance between food intake, insulin, and physical activity. If he "took it easy" and spent all his time monitoring his disease, no one would notice. But that would be boring to him.

So he runs for a hobby. He runs long distances. This requires huge effort to balance his body and keep things in check. And in his 50s he ran a marathon. Now for me, a marathon seems impossible under any circumstances. But for him it is more difficult than for most people.

There are many people who achieve these truly grand goals by overcoming challenges, and focusing, and working at it a little every day.

Financial independence is like this. You might buy a lottery ticket from time to time, but you better have other plans for your retirement. You've read the formula for financial success a hundred times: put aside a regular amount from every paycheck. $100 or $500 or $1000. Or, some say, ten percent. Do it right now. Resolve on your next paycheck to "pay yourself first" and live on $100 less per month. Just do it.

In fact, all grand goals are like this. Focus on the future you. Have a vision. Visit your vision every day. Move toward it.

Don't be discouraged. Keep going a little at a time. Don't be overwhelmed by it (in other words, relax). Simply be aware of it and move toward it. You can get there from here.

To Ponder

"The most difficult tasks are consummated, not by a single explosive burst of energy or effort, but by consistent daily application of the best you have within you."

– Og Mandino

"You can't build up a reputation on what you are going to do."

– Henry Ford

"You want to be successful? Find out what the hoops are and practice jumping.

– Karl W. Palachuk

Section II:

Where Are You Going?

At last we get to the meat! This section covers the key elements in the Relax Focus Succeed® approach. Chapter Four covers the process of goal setting and, more importantly, value setting. This is where we buckle down and do the hard work of building your personal roadmap to success.

Chapter Five is perhaps the most important piece of the book: Relaxation. The term "relaxation" isn't really accurate. I bundle together the quiet time, the relaxation, the goal-setting, and the daily process of working on your goals. Taken as a whole, this is the process that helps you to focus on your goals and bring them to life.

I almost put the current Chapter Five before Chapter Four, but I want you to begin the goal-setting process before you begin the "relaxation" process. I want you to begin outlining the values that are important to you. It's very important to have a sense of where you're going before you begin the very big project of fine-tuning.

Chapter six delves more deeply into meditation and quiet time. Here you'll find the one habit that will make all the other habits have value. Here you'll see how everything comes together, bringing consistency to the various roles you play. That in turn holds the promise for reducing stress and propelling you toward your goals.

Important Note:

We go into more detail in Chapter Five, but for now you should begin the process of taking "quiet time" for yourself every day. Here's what you need to do.

I recommend that you schedule your Quiet Time in the morning, first thing, before the rest of the house is up and about. If you need coffee to get started, go do that.

You should set aside a specific place, where you can have privacy. You'll want a comfortable chair, but probably not a big comfy chair. It should be something that allows you to sit up, be alert, and still be comfortable.

A small table next to the chair will give you a place to set your coffee or tea, as well as a small tablet of paper and a pen or pencil.

As you begin your Quiet Time, close your eyes and take a few deep breaths. This will help you adjust to a rested and thoughtful mood.

For now, you should spend your quiet time thinking about "what you want to do with your life." The notes don't have to be organized. You don't have to share them with anyone.

Later on we'll add some other activities to this Quiet Time (more formal goal-setting, etc.). At this point, just get used to the setting, and try to get in the habit of taking time – ten to fifteen minutes – every day.

Chapter 4

Values and Goals

Introduction: Assigning Priorities

To reduce stress in your life and make your work more productive, you need to take time to focus and set priorities.

If the problem is that you don't have a system to assign priorities to tasks, you might think the answer is to develop such a system. Unfortunately, that's not the answer. Simply imposing a system of priorities might do *some* good.

The real answer – the long-term answer – is to develop principles by which you run your personal and business life, and goals that are consistent with those principles. In other words, the goal is to look past today, and this week, and look at the big picture.

Every business needs a "big picture." Every person needs a big picture.

What are your goals for the next five years? The next one year? The next quarter? This day, this week, this month are all points along the way. Just as there are few straight roads, there are few straight courses to your long-term goals.

I grew up in Washington State. To go anywhere you had to go over a mountain pass. I remember as a child when I learned to read a compass and figure out which way the car was heading. I was concerned when I had to inform my father that we were heading west instead of north. Then we'd head east. Then northeast. And sometimes even south! If we need to go north, why are we going south?

He gently explained that the road had to twist and turn to get over the mountains. When the engineers build a road, they have to work around the things they can't control – like lakes, mountains, and rivers. Sometimes they change the scenery: They build bridges or tunnels, and they shore up the mountainside so the road won't slip away. But most of the time they have to work with the obstacles they have.

The road's always longer than you think it should be. But eventually it zigs and zags and gets you over the mountain. Then you zig and zag down the other side. And sometimes you find that you've spent very little time heading north. And yet you get there.

A person without a "big picture" view of where to go will always be reacting to obstacles that appear in the way. And it is very easy to get turned around and lose track of where you want to be at any given time.

All people are moving from where we've been to where we will be. Our lazy side wants to relax and stay where we are. But even if we're not steering the car, it continues to move.

So if we don't keep an eye on where we're going, we can easily get lost among the obstacles.

As a matter of perspective, we must accept that the road will take us in many directions – and that's okay. Sometimes you have to go south in order to get north. On the road to success you will have slow-downs, regulations, problems, and all kinds of other obstacles.

You need to look at the big map and plot the best long-term path. That's why you need principles to guide you and you need to write down where you're going. You need to post your principles and your goals, and you need to talk about them.

Once you have established some principles and goals, you have a mark to steer toward. And everything builds from that.

Now you can set priorities. Long-term priorities. If you need short-term priorities you should set them as well. But beware the short-term priority that interrupts your focus on the long-term priorities.

My consulting business puts a high value on technical competence and customer service. These are laid out in my company principles – they are in writing. These principles are reflected in my priorities. As a result, my company and my people make decisions with these principles in mind.

Our marketing material stresses these points. "We hire only trained and certified technicians." "Your Satisfaction is Always Guaranteed."

These principles also work their way into hiring, evaluating, and motivating employees. Every person who comes to work for us signs a contract in which I offer to pay for professional certification exams. So my people know that if they get certified by Microsoft, I'll pay for it.

This sends a very clear message that my company values technical competence. It also gives me a tool in evaluating performance.

When a job has to be reworked, it costs money and I never charge the client. Thus the client sees that they are not charged more than they are quoted, no matter how much labor is involved. And the technician still gets paid. But the technician also gets an evaluation that focuses on the right way to do the job next time. The customer gets value for their money and the technician gets educated.

My priorities in addressing a problem always put principles first. When I set up my daily, weekly, and monthly "to do" lists, my priorities always govern. Thus new problems are not automatically crises: they simply fit into the list at an appropriate place.

The process – the habit – of creating a simple set of priorities every day and every week can bring amazing clarity and focus to your work. Every morning I write down three goals for the day. One for me as a person, one for my family, and one for my business. One each. Not a long list of things to do

> At 6:00 AM every day I write down my three goals for the day. The simple process of writing them down brings clarity and focus – and reduces stress.

and details and errands. One goal for each area of my life. The complex process of dealing with the details is separate.

When you set priorities, you need to start with the "big picture," not with today. Set your "permanent" principles, then five-year goals, one-year goals, and current priorities. After that, setting daily and weekly goals is easy.

We workaholics find ourselves easily dragged back into the world of crises and short-term goals. We lose focus and perspective. We panic when the road turns south instead of looking at the map and working through the rough spots.

To reduce stress in your life and make your work more productive, you need to take time to focus and set priorities. And you can't focus unless you relax. But that's another chapter.

> Where you find consistency between your values and your actions, there you will find personal fulfillment and happiness.

Remember the old line: Work expands to fill the time available. You'll never run out of work. Making sense of it all, and maximizing your effectiveness, requires some guiding principles.

Hierarchy:
From Values to Actions

In previous chapters I have mentioned that "just" setting goals is fine for beginners. But when you get serious about improving your life and being successful, you need to start with a base and rebuild your life from A to Z.

The process is very serious but not very complicated. It starts with a base of Values or Principles. From there you build a Vision or Mission for yourself. Next, you identify the Roles you play in your life. And, finally, you examine the Activities within those roles.

All the goal-setting and behavior changes take place at this "Activities" level. This is where we find the physical manifestation of what we say we believe. Your goals, and the actions you take to reach them, are at this level.

Let's look at these layers from the foundation "up."

ACTIVITIES
ROLES YOU PLAY
MISSION / VISION
PRINCIPLES / VALUES

Values / Principles

You rarely set your values or principles. It is more likely that you simply have them. You own them (or they own you). Whether you know it or not, there are principles that govern your life. There are values that affect every decision you make.

Most of us can rattle off a dozen values that we claim to hold. It's much more difficult to sit down and go through the process of thinking about the values and beliefs that are most important to us. But this emotionally-difficult process is worth going through.

At least once every five years, you should take some of your quiet time to think about the beliefs and values and principles that matter most to you. Write them down. Work on this one day a week (for 20 minutes of quiet time) for five weeks. That should allow you enough focused attention to list five values that you really take seriously and that you're willing to list as core values in your life.

Note: Be kind to yourself. Just because you list something does not mean that you are without fault in this area. You can value a healthy lifestyle and know that there are too many Twinkies in you life. You can value friendship and acknowledge that you're not very good at maintaining contact with people.

(I'm going to use my own values and goals as the example in this chapter.)

Let's say you come up with the following five Values/ Principles:

- Honesty, Integrity

- Fairness

- Good Personal Relationships

- Healthy Life/Long Life

- Helping Others

Note: Yours may be very different. These are just examples.

Mission / Vision

Once you have a set of Values or Principles, you get to work on the single most important sentence you'll ever write: Your personal mission statement.

Once again, this takes some time. This is where you look over your values and principles and try to figure out the whole purpose of your life. That sounds dramatic. But, really, this is very valuable work.

It's very sad, but many people spend so much of their lives chasing after "goals" without examining values and having a personal mission statement. In other words, they take visible action steps to achieve things that may not be related to the things that are important in their lives.

A personal mission statement is a simple, one sentence statement of what drives you in your life. It doesn't have to be particularly profound. You can change it any time. When you boil it down to the basics, what brings value to your life?

The important rule to remember here is: Make this *your* mission statement. Make this *your* vision for your life. Do not accept "the world's" vision about success. The last thing you want is to have lots of money, no friends, a family that can't stand you, and to have a shallow, meaningless life. But that's all that can come from following other people's goals.

Your mission might be to related to your family or friends, to serving people or the community. It might be related to a cause you believe in, or to your religion. It can be anything that matters to you.

From the values listed above, you might derive the following mission statement:

My vision is to inspire success through a balance of serving myself and serving others.

Notice that the mission does not have to be a perfect match. Your values will change over time as you evolve. Your mission should also be flexible. Don't be afraid to revisit this from time to time.

There's more to cover on the subject of personal vision statements. But this is a great start. We'll revisit this topic.

Roles

The next bit of work for you is to think about the roles you play in your life. This should be much easier. Most of us play 3-5 roles. For example, I play the following roles in my life:

- Individual
- Husband
- Father
- Businessman
- Community Member

Obviously, your roles will be different.

Note that Individual is separate from me as a spouse, me as a father, etc. This is just me. Don't forget to list your role as an individual. A great deal of unhappiness comes from pretending that we don't need to tend to ourselves or acknowledge what we need independence from all the other roles of our lives.

There are other, minor roles. Looking into my life from the outside, you might see other roles than I see. But as I divide up all the various aspects of my life, these are the divisions that make sense to me today.

You are likely to have roles for you as an individual, you at work, you in a relationship, and so forth. Play with it. Change it. Rethink it.

These roles then become the basic categories for your goals. So now, at long last, we're ready for visible, physical manifestations of what matters in your life. You've defined values and principles, you've got a mission statement, and you've identified the major activity areas of your life.

Activities

Activities – the actions you take – are derived from this hierarchy of values, vision, and roles. The secret to living a happy, stress-free life is to bring the *Activities* of your life into alignment with the *values* and *vision* of your life. Stress and unhappiness are a result of conflicts between how you see yourself and how you are.

Let's take one value as an example: Generosity. If you see yourself as a generous person, but know that your actions are not generous, that causes internal stress. Perhaps you don't have enough money to be financially generous. There's no crime in that. Look at the other roles in your life.

Are you generous with your time, with your love, with your friendship?

Where you find consistency between your values and your actions, there you will find personal fulfillment and happiness.

Goals then become visible, physical actions that can be taken to bring your activities and daily life into alignment with your stated values and vision. You should examine your activities and goals for each role you play.

If you want to start moving toward greater happiness and personal fulfillment today, start identifying three goals for each role in your life. In my example, I would have three goals for me as an individual, three goals for me as a father, three goals for me as a husband, and so forth.

Summary: Values to Actions

This is a serious and time-consuming process. But it should not be difficult. And the truth is, without this entire process, you will find yourself chasing the wrong rainbows. There is no happiness or fulfillment in following someone else's dream.

This takes time. But nothing in your life is more important than determining the most important things in your life!

If you follow this process – if you take 15-30 minutes a day and work on values and vision, on defining roles and defining goals, you will automatically find yourself rethinking the actions you take every day.

You will realize that some things just don't matter. You may have been doing them for years. But now you realize they're not even on your radar. You've been working on, and stressing over things that just aren't important to you. Now you can walk away and it feels good.

You will also see where values and activities are not aligned. Perhaps you say your family is important, but you don't have time to spend with them. Writing down your values, vision, roles, and goals will put these contrasts right in front of you. Then your mind will begin doing the work of figuring out how to bring alignment to your life.

There are two options for re-aligning your life with your stated values. One is to change your behavior. No matter how difficult it may be, the process will result in greater happiness.

The other option is to rethink the values. Perhaps family just isn't as important as you thought. Perhaps "society" has made you feel guilty about not having family on the top of the list. So you put it there. Now you begin to see that it's just not your value.

Whatever you do, whatever you decide, the rewards for this work are tremendous. Take it seriously. But be kind to yourself, too. This is your life. Make the most of it.

> If you're serious about working on your vision, values, and goals, go through this section again and make a work plan. If you need help, order the Vision Quest Work Kit with audio CD from www. RelaxFocusSucceed.com.

Value Setting
The Essential Task That Makes Goal Setting Worthwhile

Let's go back and take a little closer look at the processing of setting values.

Anyone who has spent time thinking about success and happiness has also spent some time on goal setting. All too often, however, this goal setting takes the wrong approach.

> To be meaningful, your goals must be derived from your values or principles.

The first mistake that people make is to have goals that are only short term. Short term goals without long term goals are good for beginners. That is, they're better than no goals at all. But you need more. When you get serious about your life, you will need long term goals – and you'll need to know how to set them.

Let's use a boating analogy. When you begin learning how to maneuver a boat, you don't have any long term goals. In fact, it's all you can do to have short term goals: From here to the middle of the lake, over to that pier, etc. When you're starting out, all you can manage is to go from "here" to "there." Forget anything complicated like out of the bay and up the shore, let alone a major goal such as going through the Panama Canal or around the tip of Africa.

So the lesson is that you need longer term goals as well short term goals.

The second mistake people make is to have only "physical" goals. These are goals that can be seen or touched. Physical goals look something like this:

- Lose ten pounds

- Become wealthy

- Buy a new car

- Finish the book

- Increase sales 10%

There's nothing wrong with any of these goals. But actions and visible physical things tend to be reflections of the more important things they are intended to represent. Just as I cannot look at your behavior and discern your motivation, so I cannot look at your visible goals and tell which *values* they represent in your life.

For example, do you want a new car because you've never had one and this represents a level of success? Or do you want a new car because they're safer? Do you want to lose weight because you know it's good for your health, or are you just plain uncomfortable and want to get back into those jeans?

Goals (short and long term) represent values. Goals without values are really just a collection of possible activities that are truly pointless. One goal might represent one view of the world while another goal represents another view.

Most people can come up with three or four goals off the top of their heads. But ask them about the values that are important in their career and they get stuck. They can usually name a value or two for work, and maybe one personal value. Very few people can jot down 3-5 core values that they use to synthesize all the goals in their personal and professional lives.

> To be meaningful–to bring meaning into your life–your goals must be derived from your values or principles.

Establishing these "synthesizing values" is the most important work you can do to improve your life.

Imagine how wonderful your life would be if there were no conflicts between your work goals and your personal goals, between your goals as a boss and your goals as a parent. It would be spectacular, right? Then get started today!

Next Steps

The process might take some time, but there are no great mysteries here. You determine which values are most important in your life (in all aspects of your life). Then you build goals or a mission statement that applies to all aspects of your life.

The only hard parts about this process are: 1) admitting that you haven't applied values to your goals, and 2) evaluating the pieces of your life that are inconsistent with the values you now claim to be the core of your actions.

Setting Values must come before setting goals. If you say the most important values in your life are honesty, fairness, good personal relationships, a healthy life, and helping others (for example), then your goals and your actions should reflect these values.

I don't mean to make any of this sound easy. It is difficult work. It is emotionally draining work. But as I said above, it's the most important work you have to do in your life. Without this work, your life is pointless. You can steer from where you are to some other point you can see. But you can't engage in any "big adventures" because you don't know how and you'll get lost at sea.

Once you begin the process of discerning your values and establishing goals consistent with those values, you will feel stress slipping away. There are two main reasons for this. First, some things that have been bothering you will begin to iron themselves out. Problems that perplexed you will become easier to solve. You'll suddenly see that the stress you had was really due to feeling trapped in behaviors that are inconsistent with "where you want to be with your life."

Second, you will naturally change your behavior to be more consistent with your stated goals/values. That means you will stop doing some things and start doing others. You will begin to be a different person. A person with fewer internal conflicts and with greater consistency across all aspects of your life.

It takes a lot of energy to keep putting on different masks! Imagine how much easier life will be when you finally get to be the same person at all times in all places!

"One person asked me 'What if I come up with the wrong mission statement?' When I asked him what his current mission statement was, he didn't have one. I told him, 'Well, whatever you come up with will be 100 percent more accurate than the one you have now.'"
– Laurie Beth Jones, The Path

Summary and Conclusions

Please don't rush this process.

The last thing you want to do is rush into a goal-setting session, hash out a few notes, and then check it off your list.

☑ Set goals for the rest of my life

You'll want to write out your values and then revisit them. Keep going back. Test them against your daily experience. Fine-tune. Rework.

If you've been following along, you should be settling into a routine of daily Quiet Time and some work on goal-setting. We'll come back and help you fine-tune the goal setting process. Now let's look at the Relaxation part of the RFS process.

To Ponder

"Quality of Life cannot be achieved by taking the right shortcut."

— Stephen Covey

"Paths clear before those who know where they're going and are determined to get there."

— Anonymous

"Where you find consistency between your values and your actions, there you will find personal fulfillment and happiness."

— Karl W. Palachuk

Chapter 5

Relaxation And Success

Introduction

The basic formula for reaching your goals is pretty simple. First you set a goal, then you set out to achieve it. That's all good.

But those goals are often external to yourself. In other words, most goals are about you changing your world. There's very little focus on you changing you.

A truly balanced, successful, happy life requires you to spend significant energy working on you. After all, you are the most important element in your success. If you don't work on you, there are some serious limits to what you can change.

External elements are things like a comfortable retirement, a boat, or doubling your sales. Internal elements include what makes you happy, where you want to live, and who you want to spend your time with.

The *you* piece of the equation is the important part of success and happiness. Without happiness, friends, and fulfillment, the rest of it doesn't matter.

In this chapter and the next, we're going to talk about you,
and what makes you happy. We'll look at you in the past,
you in the present, and you in the future.

If you take it seriously, this can be difficult work. Emotionally difficult work. I encourage you to take this very slowly.
You might consider reading one section per day, followed
by a half hour of quiet time.

Basic Recipe for Meditation and Quiet Time

Ingredients

- You
- Comfortable Chair
- Paper
- Pencil or Pen
- This book
- Timer

Do not bring music with words. Also, no loud or
fast music.

Sit comfortably in your chair, feet on the floor.

Meditate or simply breath quietly for five minutes.

Read a section from the book.

Set your timer for 30 minutes.

Sit quietly and consider the reading. As ideas or
questions float into your mind, write them down.

It is quite natural that this material will make you feel uncomfortable, or your first reaction will be "That doesn't apply to me." I have three pieces of advice:

- Try it anyway.
- Lower your shields. Take off your armor.
- Stick to it for a month.

Be realistic: One part of you got this far in the book because you want to improve things. That requires change. Now the other part of you needs to just go along for awhile and give it a chance.

What Has Relaxation to Do With Success?

Finally, we look at the *Relax* part of Relax Focus Succeed. In the first few chapters we looked at work and workaholism. We also touched on focusing your energy. But our brains are still wired to believe that *more work* is the only way to get more done.

How can we be more productive with less work? This chapter begins that discussion.

When I'd been meditating for some time, my wife asked me if I'd like to try a yoga class with her. I told her that the thought of crawling around on the cold floor doing impossible moves was not appealing to me. She said this was different. This was hot yoga. The room is 100° F and you work out for ninety minutes.

As an aside, here a good summary for being comfortable with arthritis:

Cold = Bad   Hot = Good

So, strangely enough, this hot yoga sounded interesting to me. I said I'd give it a try. The instructor said that you need to give it a week. In other words, you can't take one class and quit. It will be too difficult, too hot, and too different from what you're used to.

The general assessment was correct. I was too hot, the yoga was too difficult, and the whole experience was too "different." But, the hot was also good. So I went back. I did it three times the first week. At that point I was hooked. Here was an exercise that kicked my butt and left me invigorated at the end.

I do not personally engage in yoga as a religious activity. But, at the same time, it is more than simple exercise. There are built-in periods of rest. One cannot be exhausted, lie flat on the floor, close ones eyes, and *not* relax.

As with many strenuous exercises, yoga keeps you moving and doing things just enough so that your mind doesn't have time to wander. As a result, you leave behind the bills and the activities. You don't think about your staff or your boss, your kids or your spouse. You're awake and alert, but your mind is engaged just enough so that it can't wander off and fixate on the troubles of life.

And so I learned that I can have quiet time, and meditative time, while moving my body.

In this chapter we explore the concept that you need to slow down in order to get more done. This is one of the key elements of any success. So much so that I've had a poster made for my staff that reads

Slow Down

Get More Done

It's true. Typing is a great example. When you learn to touch type, there's a point at which you do speed tests. Typing as fast as you can creates errors. In the old days, on a type-writer, you were simply out of luck. Now, on computers, you can backspace and fix. But, either way, if you go too fast and make too many errors, your score goes down. If you slow down just a bit, you make fewer errors. Therefore, you "get more done" by slowing down a bit.

The same is true in most activities. Relax a bit. Don't jump right in and go a million miles an hour. Be methodical. How many times have you heard "Take your time and do it right the first time?" The faster you go, the sloppier the job. Fast and sloppy equals more rework.

Now, let's explore success that's got a healthy dose of relaxation!

Clearing Up the Question of Relaxation

Perhaps the area of greatest confusion regarding the philosophy of Relax Focus Succeed® is the Relax part. After all, we live in a society that does everything but relax. We are constantly on the go-go-go. So, what do we mean by relax? Can you kick off your shoes, plop down on the couch in front of the TV, and become successful? No. Obviously not.

"Relaxation" takes in a set of activities that bring Balance into your life. It includes taking care of the physical and mental parts of your body. This includes

exercise,

true relaxation,

and time for quiet thought.

These three aspects will contribute immensely to your success.

Within these areas, you have many options. But you have to actively participate in bringing balance into your own life. No one else can do that for you. Even if they could, no one else will.

If you want to have a focused, successful life, you need to take time to take care of your body. And your mind. If you don't do these things, you can't be successful in your business or personal life. Why? Because you can't be successful if you don't know what success means to you. And that can only be achieved through balance.

What counts as relaxation?

Ah! There's the million dollar question. Let's look at the three aspects mentioned above.

The easy one is Exercise. You know what real, legitimate exercise is. If you don't, you're not being honest with yourself. You need to do two kinds of exercise: One that helps your circulation and one that helps you with strength. Some kinds of exercise do both (such as bicycling or swimming).

You need to exercise at least four times a week. It doesn't matter whether you do it in the morning or the evening, alone or with someone else. But you have to do it. The more you move your body, the longer God's going to let you keep it.

The second aspect is more difficult: True Relaxation. "True" relaxation means that you take time to let your body and mind slow down and stop "working." Perhaps the most important thing here is what doesn't count as true relaxation.

True relaxation does not include watching TV, getting lost in your hobby, golfing, reading a work-related book, playing cards, or any activity that requires your mind to be "on." Don't get me wrong: All of those activities are good, and we need to do more of them. But we also need to engage in activities that do not require the brain to be on.

True relaxation means that you're NOT engaging with other people, not letting your mind be distracted (e.g., television), and not focused on something so hard that your mind isn't actually able to think about other things (e.g., hobbies).

The point of True Relaxation is that you stop working, you stop entertaining, you stop interacting, you stop focusing outside yourself, and you begin to spend time getting to know yourself. Who are you, really? Are you happy? Do you like your job? Your friends, your car, your cat? What do you want to do with your life?

Very few people take time to stop and spend time with themselves. I firmly believe that all mid-life crises consist of people realizing that they have been running full speed ahead for twenty or thirty years without any idea where they're going. Then, suddenly, they stop and realize that they don't how they got where they are. And maybe they don't like it. And maybe they don't know whether they like it, but they resent the fact that they got there without really choosing to be there. Life pulled them along. And now, suddenly, they want to choose what to do with their lives.

With no maps, no focus, and nothing to bring meaning to their lives, too many people wake up one day and realize they haven't been participating at a meaningful level in their own lives.

Sadly, many people in this situation give up, walk away, get divorced, quit their jobs, and try to start over. Instead of looking at what is good in their lives and evaluating the right decisions they've made, they throw it all away and don't keep the even the good things they have.

So, what does True Relaxation do for you?

The first thing it does is give you time to be with yourself, to think about yourself. Second, it is a step toward contemplative thought or quiet thought.

True relaxation **does** include the following:

- Reading a book that doesn't require you to think.

- Praying or Meditating.

- Relaxing in a hot tub or similar activity that does not allow you to also do something else at the same time.

- A long walk without a walkman or someone to talk to.

The pattern should be clear. This is time you spend with yourself. You don't have to "actively" think about anything. You shouldn't be trying to work on a puzzle or fix a problem or figure out what to do about something.

You need this time because you have to get to know yourself. This is the first step toward Quiet Thought.

In True Relaxation, there is no attempt to put your life in order. There's no attempt to plan or focus. With Quiet Thought, however, there is some work. You do spend time putting your life in order, focusing, planning, and improving yourself.

Activities in this arena include Journal-writing, goal-setting, and reading books and magazines that help you improve yourself and your life.

It is very easy to see how Quiet Thought contributes to your success. Just as you need to exercise your body in order to make it last long enough for you to enjoy it in your old age, so you need to spend time exercising the contemplative side of your life.

Everyone needs to find a combination of these "relaxation" activities: Exercise, True Relaxation, and Quiet Time.

Sometimes the lines between these blur. Some exercise, for example, allows plenty of time for True Relaxation or Quiet Thought. Running without a a CD player or MP3 player is a good example. Exercise on any equipment with a bookstand is an easy combination.

You should do one of these three types of activities every day. It can be for 10, 15, or 20 minutes. Over time, you will look forward to this relaxation period and it will grow. Ideally, it will be an hour a day.

I have a reminder in my Outlook calendar that simply says "RFS" every day. Some days I do yoga, some days I ride the exercycle, some days I meditate, some days I read, some days I write or do goal-setting. But I try to do something every day.

Remember what Og Mandino says: "Form good habits and become their slave."

Be Patient with yourself! Some of these activities may be unfamiliar to you. Perhaps you've never meditated, or you don't exercise. Many people avoid quiet time with themselves because they have problems they want to avoid.

Success means attaining your goals. But first you have to set those goals. And before you can set the goals you have to know what makes you happy, and where you want to go, and what you want to do. Relaxation is about thinking, getting to know yourself, and working on becoming your future self.

For now, don't worry about how to get started. Plan to wake up 30 minutes early tomorrow. Sit in a quiet place by yourself and think about the kind of activities you want in your RFS time. Don't worry: There aren't any wrong answers. You're on your way!

Are You Too Busy To Be Successful?

Have you noticed that really successful people seem less busy than other people until you sit down and talk to them? Successful people are busy. *Really* successful people have more of an air of quiet accomplishment.

Slow Down: Get More Done

What's this difference, and how do I get it?

I think very successful people have developed a system for moving projects through to completion. Onto the plate, through to completion, and off the plate. Successful people work really hard getting things onto the plate and working the project. But they often don't have a system for getting things off their plate. These might be unfinished projects, or regular work that should be handed off to someone else.

Because we're all humans here, there are physical limits to what we can do. We can only have so many things "on our plate." Period. And when we get too many things on our plate, there's no room for even one more little thing. So we end up turning down opportunities because we literally can't do one more thing.

There are only three ways that things move off your plate: You finish them; someone else finishes them; or they become old and irrelevant and will remain unfinished forever. That third one is called failure. The second one is called delegation.

Notice that delegation equals success.

Really successful people can accomplish an unlimited number of things because they can acquire projects and have a system for moving them through to completion. They don't have to personally do everything. They just have to make sure the system works!

Really successful people have more of a sense of calm and balance because they know things will get done. They don't have lots of old, dead projects cluttering up their plate. In fact, their personal plate has a limited number of discreet projects.

Think about the process of moving a project to completion. For any project, there's a point that seems like success. It feels like you're finished. But you're not finished and you can't stop there. If you stop at the point of apparent success, you really just leave projects on your plate. We'll come back to this.

Don't Let God Make You Lazy

A Joke:

Sam was a very devout man. One day, he found himself caught in a flood. As the water was up to his knees, a neighbor came by in a rowboat and offered him a ride to safety. Sam replied "No thanks. I believe in the Lord and he'll take care of me."

The water continued to rise and Sam found himself crawling up a ladder to the roof. As he reached the roof, a Sheriff's boat came by and offered to take him to safety. But Sam told him "No thanks. I believe in the Lord and he'll take care of me."

Soon the sun began to set, darkness was all around, and Sam found himself sitting on the highest point of his roof, his feet in the water. A rescue helicopter came by and lowered a ladder down to Sam. But Sam shouted up "No thanks. I believe in the Lord and he'll take care of me."

But the waters kept rising and eventually Sam drowned.

When he got to Heaven, Sam went to God and said "I don't understand. I have tried to be a devout man. I have believed strongly and prayed constantly. And yet I am dead."

God replied "I don't understand either. I sent two boats and a helicopter."

All too often in our lives, we turn over some very important things to God or fate, believing that we can ignore important things and they'll be okay. There are many reasons for this. Sometimes, we're overwhelmed with some aspects of our lives, so we ignore other aspects. Sometimes we're lazy. Sometimes, there's just too much stress and we don't have the energy to handle "one more thing." Sometimes we're caught up in making money "today" and don't plan for tomorrow.

Several years ago, my wife and I bought one house and sold another. The details are literally overwhelming. And yet, in just a few weeks we made decisions that involve hundreds of thousands of dollars and a commitment that at least on paper will last 30 years! In this situation, we relied on professionals: realtors and lawyers and escrow people who deal with all the paperwork all the time.

Sometimes this delegation of details is appropriate. But the bottom line is that you have to take responsibility for the big picture. As my dear mother used to say . . .

"God helps those who help themselves."

Where do you turn over your responsibility and let someone or something take control in your life? Here are some danger signs. If you find yourself believing these statements, you have probably abdicated responsibility for some important aspects of your life:

- The government will take care of it. (Alternatively, "The government wouldn't let them do it if it wasn't safe.")

- My husband handles the money.

- My retirement's all taken care of (I have Worldcom and Enron stock!).

- There's plenty of time to take care of that . . .

- I'm too young (or old, or tired, or bored) to worry about that . . .

- I don't need to exercise or watch my diet, I have these pills that take care of my hypertension and diabetes.

- I don't want to think about dying and wills and probate right now.

What are you putting off that you don't want to deal with? What parts of your life have you turned over completely to someone else?

This is one of those areas in which people know what they should do and yet refuse to do it. Everyone should have a retirement plan. Social Security and the Superball Lotto are not a retirement plan. Everyone knows they need to take care of their health. But "today" I'm not going to exercise and "today" I'll get away with the double-mondo grease burger.

A great deal of what we need is simply a matter of taking a little time every day to think. We need to think about our lives. Do we have a plan? (Yes it will change, but any plan is better than no plan.)

You can begin today. Focus on yourself. Take a little time perhaps 20 minutes a day to think about where you are and where you're going. What have you turned over to others? Do you feel in control of everything? If not, what knowledge do you need to feel in control of things?

As with so many things, a daily focus on where you're going and how to get there will make every aspect of your life more meaningful. Over time you'll see a unity between who you are and who you're becoming. You'll find the "you" dealing with money and the "you" dealing with health and the "you" dealing everything else are all the same person. Your life can be rational and focused and a lot more "in control" if you just spend a little time taking responsibility for where you're going and how you want to get there.

Don't say "God will take care of me" and then not pay attention to what's going on in your life. Instead of two boats and a helicopter, maybe God sent two financial planners and an insurance salesman.

Recap.

We often find ourselves with a plateful of undone projects. Some are undone because we're avoiding them. Some are undone because we're playing martyr and doing all the work ourselves. Some are undone because we're perfectionists and no one can do the work as good as we can.

And some are undone because there are too many undone projects on the plate. We can't work in an organized fashion and we become "interrupt driven." That means we address whatever project gets thrown on our plate by the next person to walk in the door.

Unintentionally, we've created a stressful environment that sabotages our own success. We'll look at stress in a bit. But for now, how do we attack the backlog?

The first step is to make a commitment to move projects to completion. Without the commitment, don't start to make any other plans. They won't work. Really, truly, honestly make a commitment. Then you can make a plan.

The second step is to delegate some of the work. It doesn't matter what you delegate. Some projects your really do have to do yourself. But they're probably 1/10th of the number you *think* you have to do.

The final step is to build a plan for the future. Try to design a system that allows some work to automatically be done by someone else. Reduce the number of things that actually make it to your plate. Then, with the smaller number of things *on* your plate, design a process to move them off as quickly as possible.

It's important to remember that success isn't just the accumulation of dollars. Remember the exercises with values and principles. Success is filling all aspects of your life with more of the things you want.

When you don't have any strategy for moving projects to completion, then you're stuck in a stressful, reactive mode of operation. Everything's an emergency and you don't have time to

STOP!

If nothing else, use your morning Quiet Time to work on making your life more sane.

Good Stress / Bad Stress

We've all heard about "good stress" and "bad stress." I sometimes wonder whether doctors and psychologists really believe in good stress, or whether it was invented by television talk shows. I think good stress can be real, based on some events of positive stressful activities in my life.

Several times a year I am faced with a true Disaster Recovery situation with my clients' computers. For example, a hard drive fails. Very often, these jobs involve 10-15 hours of labor in one sitting. In some cases, data retrieval involves

> We deal with so much "urgency" in our jobs that we burn ourselves out.

days of work. Because loss of data is absolutely critical to clients, it can be very stressful for me.

But when it's over, I have a feeling of relief and victory. I have once again defeated "disaster" and emerged the hero. It gives me a tremendous feeling of satisfaction.

One such disaster in July 2000 stands out for me. A database was suddenly corrupted. Before I could find the cause, I needed to get the data back in shape. This involved a day's labor followed by a long phone call to the Microsoft support line for technical professionals.

In order to diagnose and fix the problem, I sat in front of the server (computer) and went through a series of steps with the support technician. He asked questions and gave advice. I had my hands on the server so I executed decisions we made and reported the results to him. The whole time, I was on the telephone with a headset so my hands would be free and my neck would not get sore.

When the call finished, the server was back up and the database was perfect again. The call was logged at 105 minutes.

When I stood up to stretch, it was like getting out of the car after a long drive. I'd been sitting in one spot with my hands on the machine, staring at the machine for an hour and forty-five minutes. It felt very much like a drive from Sacramento to San Francisco. It was a bit exhausting, but very satisfying.

There is a certain level of stress-induced energy and adrenaline at times like this. Part of me was tired and part of me was "high" on the stress and the victory.

Stress can be good. It can bring you energy. It can help your focus. And some of us don't make a distinction between this energy and the negative, destructive stress that makes our work unproductive. Negative stress destroys our personality and our lives. It makes us little work hermits who never emerge from our cubicles to enjoy the life we deserve.

If you haven't read *First Things First* (by Steven Covey, A. Roger Merrill, and Rebecca R. Merrill), you should. They present a nice division of activities into with two simple variables: Urgent/Not Urgent and Important/Not Important. So activities have the following combinations of traits:

	Urgent	Not Urgent
Important		
Not Important		

(See Covey et. al, *First Things First*, p. 37.)

Their thesis is that we spend too much time on the Urgent/ Important things and don't take the time for reflection needed to focus on those even-more-important things that are Important but not Urgent.

We deal with so much "urgency" in our jobs that we burn ourselves out.

In my work, I go to many offices and see many computers. I think one of the great inventions of our time is the fact that you can customize your P.C. I regularly come across someone who has decided to spend the afternoon re-arranging icons and adjusting the color scheme on her computer.

Invariably, the person doing this is burnt out on urgency and needs to take a "mental vacation" in which she looks busy but can spend some time doing mindless, unproductive work.

This often happens after a big push to prepare last-minute details for a meeting or presentation. In pushing people to the edge and forcing stress into the work place, many bosses see the panicky activity as work. In fact, the work is less productive than it should be and is often followed by a period of time-wasting that is invisible to the boss.

This time-wasting mental vacation can take other forms as well. Cleaning the storage closet, organizing knick-knacks on the file cabinets, etc. Even something "productive" such as filing can be a mindless task that allows a worker to take mental time off.

As with everything else, we need to tune into stress and be sure that we have a good balance. Good stress can improve productivity. Bad stress will always do the opposite. In fact, bad stress can ruin lots of co-workers' productivity as well!

Stress – Opting Out

It is very difficult to *prepare* for stress, but it can be done.

Decide now how you will react when stress happens.

You can't work on this once and be done. You have to keep working on this one.

One of the wonderful things that happens when two people get married and start their own family is that they develop their own "traditions." Her family has traditions. His family has traditions. And now *their* family develops its own traditions.

My wife and I decided several years ago that one of our traditions would be to have a Low-Stress Holiday Season. We both have large families. There are lots of people we could be running around to see. We could travel to, or through, all the major airports during the snowiest, worst, most crowded time of the year.

Or not.

So, we decided on *not*. Instead, we have a holiday with "just us." Sometimes we go someplace not-too-far-away for a few days. Sometimes a friend or family member drops by.

But opting out of the stress-filled part of the holidays is more than what we do. It's mostly about what we don't do. We don't run around like chickens with our heads cut off worrying about a perfect house for the in-laws. We don't worry about who's not getting along this year. We don't over-spend or binge.

Advice columns are overflowing with holiday advice on "dealing with" your family and friends, and getting fat, and worrying over the best toys, and spending too much. And on and on and on. Those are all potential stress events you don't have to participate in.

You might think of it as right-sizing your celebrations. You don't have to opt out altogether, but you can opt out of the things that don't bring you joy and happiness.

If you think you can't opt out, it's because you're afraid to. What will "they" think? But a little perspective should help. First, everyone opts out from time to time. You've been to those get-togethers where someone asks about a missing relative and the answer is "They couldn't make it this year." It happens. People are sorry to miss you, but generally don't obsess on why you're not there.

Second, what I call "opting out" is really putting your life in proper perspective. The reason we all need a personal philosophy and goals is so we will have them to rely on in times of stress. When you're feeling pressure between what you want to do for yourself, for your immediate family, for your friends, and for your extended family, that's the time to rely on personal philosophy and goals.

Are you living for others' expectations and don't know why? Is living for others' expectations part of your plan? It can be. There's certainly nothing wrong with it. But if you've identified the values you want to work on, and the relationships you want to improve, then the priorities fall into place.

When you make the decisions, you feel a lot more in control . . .

And a lot less Stress.

Third, you don't have to opt out of everything just the really stressful stuff. Everyone has a different tolerance level for noise, parties, running around, and general "sensory input." The holidays can be overwhelming because there's a long list of people to see, things to do, and errands that never end. We all have different personality types. Cut back to an activity level that works for you and your family.

Fourth, this is your life. Everyone will just have to get used to it. You're not closing the door on outside communications forever. You can visit people for ten other months of the year with less stress. And it will be less expensive too. And the people you visit won't be all stressed out either.

The bottom line is that you need to work toward your own personal and family goals. If you take 6-8 weeks out of the year to work on someone else's goals, that's a distraction that can set you back quite a bit. Work on your happiness; work on your family's communication; work on the things that bring you closer to God.

Don't be one of the people on the six o'clock news fighting over a $30 stuffed toy that will be on every yard sale in America next Summer!

Relax. Really.

Focus on your goals. If you don't know what your goals are (personal and family), begin working on that.

Summary and Conclusions

Relaxation is a lot easier to learn than meditation. Relaxation is naturally appealing to us. All people, in all cultures, find things to do to relax. It is a universally recognized need. Unfortunately, in our modern society, we tend not to allot enough time for relaxation.

Somehow, our norms tell us that relaxing and not working is bad, slothful, and not productive.

In truth, relaxation is vital and rejuvenating. It is an important part of success. If all you do is to focus completely on work, then what's the point of work? What are you working for?

Similarly, if you work to the point of complete exhaustion and begrudgingly take two weeks worth of vacation (at which you spend most of your time worried about the office and longing to return), then your vacation doesn't really count. You can't call that a vacation. You're checking it off the list . . .

☑ Took vacation. Relaxed.

---

but you haven't really taken a vacation and you haven't really relaxed.

As with any element of your success, you need to plan your relaxation, practice your relaxation, and give it it's proper energy and attention when the time comes. You need to learn how to relax, and how to get the benefits of relaxation.

If you work 12- and 14-hour days, seven days a week, never take time for yourself, and you're always "on" and tense, then don't take a vacation. It would be a waste of time and just irritate the people you're with.

Start by taking a day off.

Off.

Really off.

Off and not working.

Off and golfing.

Off and fishing.

Off and doing anything that's not work.

Learn how it feels. Learn to like your day off. Learn to look forward to it. Learn to love it. That way, your time off will be meaningful. It will be useful relaxation, which a stressed-out vacation is not.

Build a fun and relaxing piece into your life. That's part of the balance you need to be successful. Then, and only then, should you go on a vacation. Because then, and only then, will you have developed the relaxation muscle that makes it worth taking a vacation.

As silly as it sounds, you need to look forward to your vacation. If you work too much and are too stressed out all the time, then a vacation will just make things worse. That's not an excuse to *not* take a vacation: it is an excuse to start learning to add relaxation to your routine.

To Ponder

"Only in a quiet mind is adequate perception of the world."

– Hans Margolius

"Quiet Time is the most powerful tool you have for reaching your goals."

– Karl W. Palachuk

"There is more to life than increasing its speed."

– Mahatma Gandhi

Chapter 6

Meditation and Quiet Time

Introduction: A Consensus on Meditation

Habits, habits, habits. Good habits will make everything in your life better. Bad habits will do the opposite. One of the most important habits in your life is daily quiet time.

**Make daily relaxation a habit and
it will make you successful.**

Another great habit is collecting and reading books on success. As you read these books, take note of the role played by "quiet time," thinking, or meditation. This quiet time may be described as daily planning, daily journal writing, prayer, relaxation therapy, calming the mind, or any other practice that helps you relax.

Our cultural vision of success emphasizes power, energy, and being "on the go." Yet virtually every book on success and self-improvement speaks about taking time to stop, relax, and let your mind have time to regenerate.

If you pay attention, you will see many references to "mind-fulness," the calming mind, and the restful mind. These are the words of meditation.

"Contemplation
is the highest
form of activity."
– Aristotle

You may have a vision of meditation that includes flowing robes, a long beard, and sitting on a pillow with your legs crossed. That doesn't have to be your meditation. My personal Quiet Time involves sitting upright in a comfortable chair. I put on headphones and listen to calming instrumental music, close my eyes, and let my mind wander.

I set aside time for this practice so I don't feel rushed. I also do it first thing in the morning so it never conflicts with my day. You may wish to try relaxation tapes that talk you through relaxing your body and focusing on your breathing. You can also find guided meditation tapes that walk you through various exercises.

My experience with meditation was stop-and-go at first. It becomes easier over time. I believe that tapes or CDs help. Because I had some issues with pain, I got some recordings by Shinzen Young (see the Resources Appendix). These were particularly helpful for learning a technique that I could recreate without the CDs.

You will also find that any relaxation exercise is also a great stress-reducer.

Stress may be the most destructive force in our lives. It keeps us from having fun, it distorts our perspective, it interferes with communications, it makes us unpleasant people, it tenses our muscles and harms our bodies, and it keeps us from being successful. Stress makes focus difficult.

You have no enemy greater than stress. And you have no tool more powerful than relaxation and meditation. Meditation brings strength and focus, calmness, happiness, physical health, and success. Meditation brings it all together:

Relax - Focus - Succeed

There are an unlimited number of ways to relax. Find them. Try them. See what works for you.

Make daily relaxation a habit and it will make you successful.

Contemplation

Somewhere between relaxation and focus is the stage I call *contemplation*. It's really the first step in focusing. Perhaps the single most important step in the evolution of your success is to begin the commitment to contemplation.

Contemplation begins with time spent letting your mind wonder wherever it wants.

As a kid I had a series of paper routes. I discovered a great joy in a certain level of "mindlessness" that goes with the job. I would walk or ride my bike, and for an hour or two every day I had time to think. Just think.

My mind wandered about. Sometimes I thought about school, my parents, girls, a customer I might run into, toys. Anything. Whatever came to mind, that's what I thought about. When I was a little older I had jobs in the orchards of central Washington State. Picking and sorting fruit definitely gives one time to think!

I haven't had many jobs since then that have afforded me this luxury. Once in awhile I have a mundane task. Yard work is often good for just thinking. So is painting when I need to do that.

But I no longer have a job that allows me time every day to just think for an hour.

I have a simple problem-solving device that comes from my paperboy days. First I formulate the problem. Then I set it aside and do something else. If I can, I take at least a day. In the back of my mind, the problem sits, waiting to be solved. I usually find that answers begin to present themselves when I'm doing something else. And it's usually when I'm doing something mundane and my mind is not actively working on something else.

I've had days of doing "nothing" that resulted in ideas to solve a dozen problems. I remember once cleaning the garage and painting a workbench. Then suddenly I found myself laying out a network security system that had been vexing me for some time.

It's a shame that our society teaches "serious" business people to look down on leisure time. Your brain needs time off to sort things out.

Set yourself a goal: Make time to just sit and think. Do it away from your desk. Relax. Close your eyes. Listen to instrumental music.

As you work your way through this book, I hope you will be drawn to the habit of relaxing and contemplating. Once you

begin, you will proba-
bly become addicted.

For now, set it as a
goal. Try to do it once.
Then do it again.
Eventually find time
several times a week.
Then make time
every day.

> Perhaps the single
> most important step in
> the evolution of your
> success is to begin the
> commitment to relaxation
> and contemplation.

Introduction to Retreats

In the Monty Python movie The Holy Grail, King Arthur's
men do not use the terms "charge" and "retreat." Instead
they use "charge" and "Run away! Run away!" So, when
I tell my wife I'm going on my annual retreat, she always
says "Run away! Run away!"

Part of me wants to say that I'm not running away. But the
truth is, I am. As a part of modern society, a piece of me feels
a little guilty about "abandoning" my family and work and
all the chores that need to be done around the house. This is
particularly acute since my retreat comes in the early part of
December. I'm also abandoning putting up lights, shopping
for gifts, and holiday parties. But perspective helps (as it
always does).

Sometimes we need to "run away" from everything. To retreat
is to withdraw, to enter seclusion. Is the holiday season a bad
time for a retreat? Maybe. But when's a good time? Maybe
the holiday season is the perfect time to step back, take time
for yourself, and plan for the next year.

There are many benefits to be gained from a retreat. The most obvious are Rest and Relaxation. On one retreat I attended, the leader asked people as they were gathering together whether they'd taken time for a nap. "What's the point of going on retreat," he asked, "if you're not going to take a nap?"

Many people find that it takes time–twelve hours or more– to quiet themselves and leave the world outside, and to focus on being away from it all. And then the end comes too quickly. We are a society completely deprived of quiet time and solitude. Going on a retreat forces solitude upon you. And then you become hungry for it. With luck, you incorporate quiet time into your life.

Retreats are also a time for thinking and planning and goal-setting. Who am I? What's my purpose here on Earth? What do I want to do? How do I get there from here? Focusing is very difficult without time to relax. On a retreat you will have time to think; time to straighten out problems; time to plan for the future; time to put things in perspective.

And perhaps time to respond to a subtle call from God.

There are many kinds of retreats. The first step in finding a retreat that's right for you is to consider . . .

What's your goal? What kind of retreat are you looking for?

Couple focused

Educational

Health/Fitness

Meditation

Men- or Women-focused

Personal Development

Re-energizing

Relaxing

Religious

Renewal

Yoga (spiritual or exercise)

Other?

Once you begin considering what you want from a retreat, you can start looking for one that's right for you. How do you find one? Most retreats have some religious or spiritual component, so the first place to look is at the office at your church, synagogue, or temple. There may be flyers or advertisements on a bulletin board, or someone may know who to call.

You can also search on the Internet. If you put the words "retreat" and your city/county in a search engine, you're likely to come up with something. A few sites that can help you find retreats almost anywhere are:

www.retreatfinder.com

www.findthedivine.com

www.passionist.org

Just remember that these are NOT comprehensive listings. Almost every city and county has many retreat opportunities. You just have to look.

Can you create your own personal retreat of one? Of course. As you might imagine, I encourage this. But it is best to go on a guided retreat (especially a silent one) before you create your own personal retreat. They will provide you with hints and tips, and probably some good readings, that will help you see the full benefits of a retreat.

Then you can "run away" whenever you need to.

Meditation and Prayer

The Silent Monk
(A Joke)

> Brother John joined a monastery where the brothers were only allowed to speak two words every five years. After he'd been at the monastery five years, the head Friar called him into his office and asked which two words he would like to speak.
>
> Brother John said "Bed hard." The Friar nodded his head.
>
> Five years later, Brother John was once again called into the Friar's office. "Brother, which two words would you like to speak?" he asked. Brother John said "Food bad." The Friar nodded.

Again, five years passed and Brother John found himself in the Friar's office. When asked which two words he would like to speak he replied "Chapel Cold." And the Friar nodded.

Still another five years passed. Brother John was called into the Friar's office. When asked which two words he had chosen to speak, Brother John said "I Quit."

The Friar nodded and said "I'm not surprised. You've done nothing but complain since you got here."

Some people have an uneasy feeling when they hear the word "meditation." This is probably because it doesn't sound like a comfortable part of our Western view of the world. Some people wonder whether it is un-Christian.

In fact, meditation is very much a part of our cultural history and in fact very Christian. Most commonly, we think of Buddhism when we think of meditation. But, as the joke above illustrates, we also recognize that a silent, ascetic lifestyle is part of western tradition. After all, Moses, Abraham, and Jesus all went off to pray quietly, alone.

If you are interested in finding out more about the Christian history and practice of silent meditation, read *Moment of Christ* by John Main.

Perhaps the most intriguing element of meditation (and most difficult for most of us) is that this is not you talking to God; it is a time to listen to God. It takes time and patience to learn to quiet your mind. We tend to want to be active participants (asking God for things or thanking God for things). Sometimes you have to let God do the talking.

This transition from talking (asking) to listening requires humility.

The great Thomas Merton believed that we need humility to stop acting like children and start behaving like adults. Children are intensely egotistical. They believe the world was created to serve them–to bring food and toys, to provide comfort, and generally to make sure everything is "right" in their world.

As adults we need the humility to realize that we exist as part of a larger world. Our role is not to take and take and take, but to give our share as well as take our share.

Perhaps you've heard the phrase "It's not about you." It takes humility to realize that almost nothing in the known universe is about you. It's actually a bit of a depressing thought at first. But after some reflection you realize that "It's about others." It takes humility to think about others instead of ourselves. It takes humility to serve others, help others, feed others, and love others.

If "it" were about you, whatever it is, then when you pass on, it will simply cease to exist. But if "it" is about others, then it will live forever. It is bigger than you and better than you and more powerful than you. That takes humility. But it needs you to participate and make it possible. It needs you to help others, share with others, teach others, respect others, love others, and be an example for others.

Success and the Monkey Mind

Let's say that you want to try relaxing and maybe a little meditation. You'll find that it's difficult at first, not because there's anything difficult in the process, but because you just can't sit quietly.

Our modern society makes us into people who don't feel "alive" unless they're distracted. One time, as I was preparing for a 3-day silent retreat, my daughter asked about the silent part. "If you can't talk," she asked, "what's the point of living."

Unfortunately, that attitude permeates our lives. We live in a culture that is always "on." We watch TV while browsing the Internet, text messaging, and glancing over at the email that just popped onto the screen.

> Are you too busy to be successful?

We're so completely distracted, it's a miracle that we get anything accomplished.

Our minds are frequently "busy" with many (seemingly) disconnected thoughts. When we try to sit and focus, we are constantly bombarded with ideas and problems and random ideas.

When meditating, this is particularly disruptive. Buddhist monks refer to this very-busy mind as having "monkey mind." It is worst when one first begins learning to meditate. It takes practice to learn to quiet the mind.

But monkey mind can also have harmful effects on other aspects of your life. If you just want to sit and read, or spend some quiet time on a project, your monkey mind can be there making it difficult to concentrate. And, of course, we've all had the experience of being completely exhausted yet unable to sleep. When that happens, we tend to find ourselves going over problems, bills, hassles, etc. "Monkey mind."

Some are quick to point out that a "monkey mind" can also be an active, creative, whirl of ideas that lead to tremendous creativity. It can lead one to see connections that others cannot see.

I suppose all of that's true. The monkey mind can be distracting and the monkey mind can be creative. I'm interested in the question: How does the monkey mind affect your success?

Most successful people are used to juggling and balancing and trying to do "a million things at once." Naturally, if you were to sit down and find some quiet time, you would be overwhelmed by these million things.

Yet we know that sitting quietly and taking time to consider the day before us – consider our plans and goals – is a critical element of success. Having a monkey mind is natural in this instance. It is completely expected and is really just one more thing you have to be aware of.

Here are seven ways that monkey mind can affect your success:

First, daily quiet time will be difficult for someone with an active, monkey mind. This is true of meditation, prayer, or just a half hour of solitude. But this is only true at first. If you've never taken the time to spend quiet time by yourself, you'll feel strange. You'll be overwhelmed by a sense that you should be doing something, not just sitting there.

It is important to believe that just sitting there is doing something. It is the hard work that has to be done to accelerate your travel on the road to success.

Second, an extremely active mind can lead to an extremely active person. But that doesn't mean your actions are fruitful and constructive. If you hang around a daycare you'll see very active kids running and jumping, throwing balls and singing

> "Don't Just Do Something . . . Sit There!"

songs, laughing and fighting. (And that's before recess!) What you see is a whirl of activity. My mother referred to it as blowing off steam. It's really just doing "something" because there is so much energy you can't do "nothing."

But beware of falling into the belief that doing *something* is constructive and useful. Doing something unproductive just so you don't have to sit doing nothing is not an appropriate motivation. Even as an extremely active person, your time and energy are limited. You need to be disciplined about spending your time in productive ways. Many people have written books on organizing priorities. Rather than spend your time wasting your time, read a book!

Third, you need to overcome monkey mind in order to relax. And you need to relax in order to do the important work of focusing, setting goals, setting the agenda for today, evaluating your life and business. Relaxation is an extremely important part of success.

Relaxing won't be easy for you. It may for other people, but not those with monkey mind. Which means that you will have to work at it. You have to practice relaxing. You have to get used to that feeling and stick with it long enough to become comfortable with it and find value in it.

Fourth, your active mind will make the sorting of priorities more difficult. After all, if you have a million thoughts racing through your mind, picking the ten most important things and sorting through them in order is a monumental task. Perhaps the first chore is to practice recognizing what does not need to be done (or does not need to be done by you). As with all behaviors, you need to develop the habit of sitting quietly to sort through priorities.

The Fifth effect follows from the Fourth: Recognize that you will be bombarded with ideas–even great ideas–and that they are not all worth pursuing. You need to set a threshold for your actions. When is an idea, invention, financial pursuit, or opportunity worth your time? The criteria are up to you. There may be emotional value in one activity and financial value in another.

Your decisions don't have to be "rational" by anyone's standards, but they do have to be your decisions. You can't do everything. Period. Stop trying. Do selected things very well.

Sixth, recognize that for most people who have a very active mind, the monkey mind will never go away. And making it go away will not be your goal. The important work then becomes practicing quiet time on a regular basis so that you tame this thing. Monkey mind is not a bad thing. It is not a "monster." In your case, it is a key to your success and your creativity. But it does need to be tamed. With quiet time, relaxation, and focus, you can channel these thoughts into meaningful actions. Instead of a whirlwind of just plain activity, focus your actions into a whirlwind of productive actions.

Seventh, with an active mind it becomes much more important to spend some quiet time writing. You should write out your goals by hand once a month. This makes them personal. And you know your mind: you won't just transcribe them. You'll fine-tune and tweak and clarify. Again, this is important work for you. Writing forces you to stop and think. It makes you clarify. It forces a level of commitment, even if you never share it with anyone.

What's Next?

The obvious question is "What should I do?" I can't answer that. If you recognize that you have a monkey mind, you need to do the hard work of making something useful of it.

Every life should have value and meaning. Every person should have goals and work toward them. People with active minds tend to have too many goals and that can lead to not pursuing any of them in a meaningful way.

Any place you start will be a good place. It should involve some quiet time. Be patient with yourself. This really is hard work.

"You have to stop in order to change direction."
– Erich Fromm

And don't forget to enjoy this work. After all, you're changing your life for the better. That's good stuff. It is exciting and important work, and you should have a good time doing it.

Kick-Starting Your Meditation

At the beginning of Chapter Five I gave a "Basic Recipe for Meditation and Quiet Time." Review that again.

In Chapter Twelve, we'll cover some exercises to get you moving toward a Relax Focus Succeed plan of your own. But for now, I'd like to send you on a shopping trip.

Please go to the local bookstore and find the audio programs section. Look through the titles on relaxation, meditation, breathing exercises, etc. It's sometimes hard to know what to pick until you've already listened to a few. But do the best you can.

Here's what you're looking for: a CD that has guided meditations. It should be calming and soothing. Don't buy one filled with philosophical lectures on the benefits of meditation. You're looking for actual meditations.

Spend $15 or $20 on a CD. Don't buy a big 6-CD pack until after you've listened to a 1-CD pack and decided that you really like the person's style.

Once you have your CD, set up your morning quiet time station with a CD player (or MP3 player) and headphones. Settle in and enjoy a daily guided meditation. Anything from 15-30 minutes is great to start out. After awhile you might stay for 45-60 minutes.

Guided meditations are great for beginners because the voice draws you in and keeps your attention focused. Without that, sounds and thoughts float into your mind and you have to consciously set them aside.

Here are a few more tips for success:

- Some local libraries have great audio collections, and many even have MP3s. Check that out and save yourself some money. If you find one you just have to own, go buy it.

- If you have a special need (e.g., stress or pain), look for a meditation that addresses that need.

- Look online for sources. This is particularly helpful after you find someone you like. It is very likely that they have more CDs online than you'll find in the store. One place to start is www.audiobooksonline.com.

> If you would like an audio program to get your started on a basic relaxation meditation, go to http://www.relaxfocussucceed.com. Go to the Books/Audio section and click on the link for the Free Quick-Start Guided Meditation. This is in MP3 format and you will need an MP3 player.

Summary and Conclusions

Perhaps the most difficult piece of the Relax Focus Succeed® process is the Relax part. I have made presentations for years, asking people to just try it. Almost no one does.

In my presentations I say this: Try it for thirty days. Start tomorrow. Take fifteen minutes of quiet time every day for thirty days. You don't need an agenda. You don't need music or workbooks. All you need is you. Sit by yourself and just allow yourself fifteen minutes of quiet time.

I promise that, if you do this every day for thirty days, it will have a noticeable, positive impact on your life. For some people, it will have a dramatic positive impact.

The process won't be easy at first. But nothing's easy at first.

Eventually, if you stick with it, this quiet time is addictive. For many people, it's the first time as adults that they've been by themselves, sitting quietly, paying attention to their goals and their dreams.

Please try it. Please add this to your daily routine. Give it an honest try for thirty days and let me know how it goes.

To Ponder

"A light heart lives long."
— William Shakespeare

"Attention–focus–is the most important element in your success today and every day."
— Karl W. Palachuk

"Constant Fine-Tuning is the true path to wisdom, so learn a little every day."
— Jack Canfield, Mark Victor Hansen, and Les Hewitt

"Form good habits and become their slave."
— Og Mandina

Section III:

Working the Plan

I think that some people never get started on goal-setting and working on their future because that process simply has no meaning for them. We're told "You have to set goals." We hear it again and again and again.

But goal setting takes time. And if you've never experienced the success that comes from setting a path, focusing like a laser beam, and making it happen, then goal setting is just an idea.

Wade Cook wrote a good book called *Don't Set Goals (The Old Way)*, designed to help people who don't like the old, standard goal-setting process. I have a different approach, but it addresses the same problem.

If you're going to be successful at creating a vision for yourself and making it come true, then it has to be an intensely personal process that you design and you enjoy.

I hope you've had the experience of falling in love with a plan, project, or scheme. It's one of the greatest, most energizing things that can happen in your life. You wake up filled with energy, and everything you see and do seems somehow related to your project.

You take on business plans and Excel spreadsheets in pursuit of the details. You're motivated and excited. As a result, you jump in with both feet and the project advances at great speed.

In that scenario, goal setting is not a sterile process you "have to" do. No, goal setting is simply another exciting part of the big project. It is great fun, and it also gives you energy.

In such circumstances, we learn the real value and place of goal setting.

The key to making this process exciting is that it's *personal* and directly related to what you want to do. In the following chapters we're going to look at dreams and goal setting, and putting your future success in the context of your whole life, past, present, and future.

After that we look at two more pieces of the big picture: motivation and physical activity. Why? Because the big picture requires a little time on each piece. You need to maintain motivation. You need to stay healthy.

Remember, that "big picture" is you with a totally balanced, happy, successful life – both personal and professional.

Chapter 7

Setting the Stage for Working on You2

Introduction

Let me introduce the next person you will become. We're going to call this person You2. As you recall from Chapters One and Two, I believe that we need to have a vision of ourselves as evolving people.

I said that we've all been many people. You're not the same person you were five years ago, and you're not the same person you'll be five years from now.

You get to decide whether the next version of you – You2 – evolves as a response to the world around you, or whether you actively mold that person into the person you want to be. Obviously, I encourage you to take an active role in deciding what you future looks like and how you're going to get there.

Just one note before you dive in: Make a note to yourself right now that you don't have to feel guilty about all this focus on You. This process involves you thinking about you, and what makes you happy, and where you want to go.

There's nothing wrong with that! It's not selfish to work on your personal life. In fact, one of the universal outcomes of this process is that you'll spend more time with people who love you, you'll have a better family life, and everyone around you will benefit from your balanced perspective.

While we're going to focus on "You," the changes that take place will be the same as if we'd spent time on your successful marriage, your successful parenting, your successful managing, etc.

We start with this very moment in your life and proceed to look at the Future You – the You2 – that will come from the process.

Focusing on the Moment

> Focus on the Here.
> Focus on the Now.
> React to the reality in front of you:
> Not to the emotional history behind you.

Throughout this book you'll see references to "focusing" on your success. Lots of books have been written on the concept of focusing on the moment, but I want to relay an incident that made this point very clear to me.

I take Bikram-style yoga classes several times a week. This is a special type of yoga consisting of 26 poses in a hot room (about 100 degrees). Each class takes 90 minutes.

Awhile back I was in a 6 AM yoga class. About half way through, the instructor said to me "I'd like to see a little more effort there, Karl."

My first thought was, "Hey! I got up in the middle of the night to be here for a 6 AM class! I've done 45 minutes of strenuous exercise and I'm about to do another 45 minutes of strenuous exercise! In a room that's 100 degrees! There are only four other people here! I've already put out the effort."

After a little reflection, of course, I had a different perspective. All those things were true. But, after all, I was there to exercise. And I'd gotten up in the middle of the night to go to a 6 AM class in order to do myself some good. So I actually had many reasons to put in a little extra effort at that moment.

The lesson is simple: You have the ability at any moment–at *every* moment–to put out a little extra effort. When you find yourself in a meeting you want to escape, or at a cocktail party you can't handle, or performing a dreary task at your desk, that's the moment to focus on your success. You are in the situation: Make the best of it. Put out a little more effort. Then move on to the next moment of your success.

In the same vein, you have the power, at every moment, to take a breath and consider whether your first reaction to a situation is the reaction you wish to exercise. *You experience your life one moment at a time.* Being aware of that, and experiencing it at a conscious level, will give you many more opportunities for success.

So, let's see a little extra effort out there.

Dream Elaborately

You've certainly heard the advice that you should "Dream Big." True enough, but you should also dream elaborately. In fact, you should daydream elaborately. Here's why.

Dreams are wonderful things. I sleep very soundly and rarely remember my dreams. Perhaps that's why I feel comfortable daydreaming (so I don't miss out on all the fun).

Dreaming – especially daydreaming – is one of those activities too quickly dismissed by our "success-focused" society. But daydreaming is a great way to strengthen your muscles of success.

I don't mean casual dreaming. I say:

Dream Elaborate Dreams!

> You need to work the muscles of success – including the dreaming muscle.

We hear over and over again the power of visualizing our goals. You know the routine: "See yourself as the president of your own company . . . or the president of Microsoft . . . or President of the United States."

Elaborate dreaming is like that kind of visualization—multiplied by 100! Here's an example.

Let's say your dream is that you want a new house. The casual dream is that you want a house big enough for your music collection, with a nice backyard.

The elaborate dream is that you can see yourself walk through the house. Is it in a brand new neighborhood, or a bit older with lots of trees? Perhaps an old Victorian. Or something in the middle. What does the entryway look like? What shelves and plants will you place there? What color is the kitchen? How will you fix it up?

The difference is obvious. As you dream elaborately, you visualize all the details. And as you go through the details – the walls, the floors, the fireplace, bookshelves, lamps, etc. – the house becomes more real to you.

Elaborate dreaming has several advantages. First, the rich detail makes your house seem that much more real in your mind. Instead of casual "someday" dreaming with words such as "I could" or "I might," you begin to think "I will." This positive attitude will help to make your dream come true.

Second, elaborate dreaming helps you to look at the realities of your dream. Rather than a nondescript, amorphous dream, you begin to see the specific positive and negative aspects of your dream. And while we are reluctant to include these "negatives" as part of our dreams, they are very important to making the dreams come true. As you begin to consider the cost of painting and furniture, the real cost of your dream begins to come into focus.

One of the most common reasons for failure in any venture (business or personal) is under-estimating the cost. When planning a business, or a vacation, or a remodeling job, we tend to look at a few big numbers and ignore all the little ones. For example, we look at the cost of the house, but not the new tile, the paint, the shelving, etc.

The third benefit of elaborate dreaming is that you get used to the details of the dream. Just as you'll get used to living in the new house. Having a detailed vision of what you want makes house shopping and buying much easier. You'll be able to walk into a house and know in five seconds whether it's a contender.

And when it's time to bargain for a price, you'll have a realistic sense of how much extra work it will take to become your "dream home." If it will take a lot of work, you'll be less willing to give in on the price.

There are many other examples as well. If you are a business owner and thinking of hiring a new person, consider every aspect of the new position: Salary, office space, candidate temperament, etc. The more you "know" about the position, the better able you'll be to find the candidate, assign an appropriate salary, and fit this position into the overall company.

> "Happy are those who dream dreams and are ready to pay the price to make them come true."
> – Leon J. Suenens

Elaborate dreaming is a great way to keep your mind busy and active. Rather than be a couch vegetable (with your mind turned off), spend your time actively working out the details of your next great venture. This is true for hobbies such as woodworking, weaving, and gardening. It works just as well for business-related sales plans, workflow, and marketing.

Casual dreams never come true.

Why? Because there's nothing to work on and there's nothing to work toward. With elaborate dreaming, you begin to divide the big dream into smaller pieces. As you consider the details, you become immersed in the project. As you identify the pieces, you identify tasks that can be accomplished.

All Dreams that Come True

Are Elaborate Dreams

This follows logically. As you begin to actually make your dream come true, you will have to deal with the details. You'll develop a plan, a budget, and a timeline. You will do all the work necessary to make all the details come together. At some point it stops being "the dream" and becomes "the project." By the time the project is finished, someone has dealt with all the details.

The more details you work out beforehand, the better the outcome.

So begin today! Dream elaborately. Even if you end up not making every dream come true, you need to work the muscles of success–including the dreaming muscle.

Have a good time.

The Past Behind You

What pushes you up and what pushes you forward?

Focus on that and thrive!

We all have some analogy we use for goal setting and looking to the future. Some say there's a point or place we move toward. For some it's a journey or a road with winding turns. For others it is a series of goals and decisions that drive us forward.

But what about your past? The older I get, the more I realize that people's past has a tremendous effect on their present and future. Of course, the older I get, the more past I have!

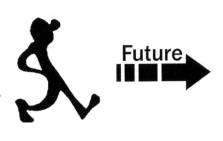

If your future lies in front of you, then your past can occupy one of these places:

Beneath You

Above You

Behind You

The Past Beneath You consists of the experiences that support you. These are the successes you've had; the love of your family and friends; things that build your self confidence.

It's a wonderful thing when people have a loving, supportive, positive childhood because this gives them a very strong, supportive "past" to sustain them throughout life. When children don't grow up with that support, they need to build other experiences and successes to support themselves.

It is very important that we stop from time to time and make note of our successes. As we experience successes in all areas of our lives, we need to consciously add them to the list. Every month, every year, we build and reinforce this structure beneath us.

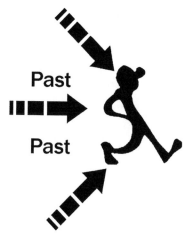

In this way, those who have a past with little or no support can build their own past – and their own support structure. The primary requirement is to focus on the events in our lives and choose to make note of the successes. We choose to view today's success as tomorrow's "support."

The Past Above You consists of all the things that hold you down. These include negative experiences, lack of education or certification, or a poor sense of self-worth.

None of this is permanent. None of this is your future. None of this is relevant to your life today.

The past above you can be a great source for goals in your life. When I talk to people about the negative thoughts in their lives I often hear them say "I don't know how much of this is real and how much is me." For example, if I feel I've been insulted, I might feel negative reactions but not know whether the other person intended something negative. I could be reacting to my past as much as to the present (often, more than the present).

You have the power to re-interpret the past. More importantly, you have the power to interpret things positively today, as they happen.

How do you escape the "past above you" so it will not hold you down? The most important thing you can do is to focus on today, on this moment. Believe that today, when you make a choice, you are free from the past. Choose to be free. Get in the habit of ignoring the past that keeps you down.

> It is your choice to dwell on the past or focus on the future.

Another great strategy for escaping the past that keeps you down is to move *fast*. It's a simple matter of physics: The power pushing down on you will have less effect as your forward motion increases. This makes perfect sense. After all, when you focus on your goals, and the future, you are less likely to be distracted by the past. The faster you move toward your goals, the less relevant are the negative thoughts and experiences of your past.

When you focus on success, you build "past" experiences that support success and support you. So as you create more experiences of success, you build a stronger foundation of success under your feet and the past that wants to keep you down becomes weaker and weaker.

Work on the negative in a positive way. Perhaps the past that keeps pushing you down is a social or educational barrier. What a great place to start building your success: Simply re-interpret your barrier into a goal. You lack the education? Then your goal is to educate yourself! You "don't know anyone in the business?" Then your goal is to find and meet someone "in the business."

It may be that the barrier you have to overcome is huge. It may even seem overwhelming. But re-define it into a goal and you will begin to create a vision and a plan.

Problems–barriers to success–are only overwhelming until you begin to take them apart and work on each little piece. Remember how the ant eats an elephant: one bite at a time.

Again we see the need to constantly read books and listen to CDs that focus on success. The more you read, the more you'll come across stories of people who overcame seemingly-hopeless odds. You must believe that you can overcome any barrier. Decide you will, then build a plan.

The Past Behind You consists of those things that push you forward. This includes anyone who tells you "you can do it" or "I'll help." More importantly, it consists of your desires and dreams. These are all things that motivate you and drive you and compel you.

Again, you get the opportunity to re-examine the events behind you. The Past Above You is also behind you, pushing you forward–if you see it that way.

The Past Beneath You does more than support an old you: It is behind you, pushing you forward as it supports you.

There is very little in our lives that is truly "neutral" in nature. Virtually every experience we have must be interpreted as positive or negative. And *you* get to make those interpretations! Is The Past Behind You just the past, or is it

The Past Beneath You, pushing you forward and supporting you?

You get to choose.

> "Forget the past.
> No one becomes
> successful in the past."
> – Anonymous

Choose to interpret your past positively. Choose to move fast so that the forces holding you down have less of an effect over you. The faster you move to the future, the more you realize that you control the forces around you. The future is constantly flowing upon us and becoming the "the past."

As you take control of your life and interpret events, you literally create your past anew every day.

You've heard people say "Someday we'll look back on this and laugh." Why wait? Begin interpreting your past as soon as it happens. Put a positive spin on it, too.

Building the Future

So, as we've seen, there are three forces from the past:

- The Past Beneath You

- The Past Above You

- The Past Behind You

The Past Beneath You consists of the experiences that support you. These are the successes you've had; the love of your family and friends; things that build your self confidence.

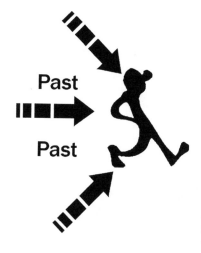

The Past Above You consists of all the things that hold you down. These include negative experiences, lack of education, or a poor sense of self-worth.

The Past Behind You consists of those things that push you forward. This includes anyone who tells you "you can do it" or "I'll help." More importantly, it consists of your desires and dreams. These are all things that motivate you.

From time to time I'll read an interview with someone famous and come across the question "What makes you get up in the morning?" That's a great way to look at the forces pushing you forward. If your answer is "I don't know" or a generally un-impassioned summary of your dull, dreary life, then you need to re-evaluate your life!

You need goals and dreams and passions to push yourself forward.

What should you do if you don't have people and forces pushing you forward? Start to acquire them! Your past is a very powerful thing: use it,

> All the forces push you forward. Some up, and some down. But there are no forces pushing you backward.

manipulate it, and make it work for you!

Begin today. Build experiences, goals, and relationships that push you forward. Find people who support and encourage you. Set some goals and share them with someone who will hold you accountable. Make arrangements to exercise with someone else.

Focus on the past that supports you.

So much for the past. Now let's look at the future. Before we get too far, I want to make one thing very clear: There are no forces holding you back.

Remember that the forces in your life consist of *experiences* and how you *interpret* them. All of your experiences are in the past.

The only forces that "work against you" are the forces that hold you down. And, as we've seen, they only have this influence because you decide they do.

There are no forces holding you back.

So what's in front of you? For the most part, the support in front of you consists of your faith or belief that a support system will be there.

The support system consists of your talents, your friends, your contacts, your family, your skills, and all those things that look a lot like the Past Behind You. Except this is in front of you. These are experiences and actions that haven't been experienced yet.

Let me give an example. I have many experiences building computers. I know which screws go where, what to watch out for with wiring, and so forth. New technology comes out all the time, but the fundamental tasks connecting hardware devices doesn't change much. My talents serve me well. There is no stress for me when I open a computer case, nor is there concern that I won't be successful.

Many other activities in our life are the same way. If you have a lot of experience on a particular job, you know every aspect of that job. You know how things work and feel. You know when it's right and when it's wrong.

Think about any skill or ability you have that you do well. Your ability to work fast and do well relies in large part on your experience about how things work. You believe the wood (or cloth or pipe or whatever) will act a certain way because of your experience.

And when you do something that you've done a thousand times before, you know what to expect. It's like taking that next step, even though the experiences of your past may not be right there supporting you. But you believe that the entire support system is there.

And it is. Your current experiences become the Past Beneath You very quickly, supporting your next step.

Many people are afraid to move forward with any measure of speed because they lack the faith that their support system will be there. They don't believe that, when the next footstep comes down, there will be something under it to hold them up.

It is particularly difficult to move forward quickly because that requires even more faith. To move quickly, we have to believe that our support system is strong enough, and will continue to be strong enough, to support us when we're fully committed. When you're fully committed, you can't stumble backward. You have to have something there to support you.

You can see where faith comes in. When you're moving slowly, you have lots of time to build a stepping stone before you put your foot in front of you. When you move quickly, you just have to believe that your system works. Friends will be there, family won't let you down, your talents are sufficient, and so forth.

So, how do you build this system of support? The basic building blocks are talent, integrity, and hard work. If you want friends, you need to cultivate them. If you want skills, you have to learn and practice. If you want positive experiences, you have to make them happen.

You have years of experience. That's one step you can count on. You have talent and ability. That's another step. You have your last success. That's one more step. Friends and family are a step or two. See how it works? As you tally up your past successes, they become the foundation for future success.

It's the same old story: If you've built a world of faith and support, of talents and skills, then those things will be there every step along the way. And the more you work on your personal support system, the more faith you'll have that you can take the next step, and the next, and the next.

As your faith and your support system grow, you can increase your speed, knowing that the next step will not falter. You have the talent, the experience, the friends, etc. Whatever you need, you've built a system that allows you the freedom to take the next step without worries.

Moving quickly also removes some of the pressure from the past above you – those things that try to hold you down. When you're moving forward, and focusing on the positive experiences that make the next steps possible, the forces from the past are less effective at pushing you down.

Summary and Conclusions

Perhaps success isn't an endpoint at all, but a state of faith in which you believe the next step is more than merely possible: You believe that the next step on your journal will be exactly as you need it to be. And the next. And the next. And the next.

So, ultimately, success consists of building a system that will support you as you make your way along life's journey. No matter where you go or what you do, it's there to support you. Your past experiences have combined to create a path to future success that cannot fail.

I believe this is true for all of us, and I believe it's never too late to start. Begin now building the past that will create the support system that leads inevitably to your future success!

To Ponder

"The best place to succeed is where you are with what you have."
                              – Charles M. Schwab

"The past, the present, and the future are really one: they are today."
                              – Harriet Beecher Stowe

"Success is not an endpoint: It's a process of moving in the direction you want to go."
                              – Karl W. Palachuk

Chapter 8

Working On Your Goals

Introduction
Focus on Success

In the most basic sense, to focus means to put your attention on something. But focus is not a simple thing.

At times you will use focus to mean goal-setting. Other times, having established your goals, you will use focus to mean deciding on a course of action. And yet again, when you look at the "big picture" and evaluate where you've been and where to go next, focus will be the measuring stick to evaluate your progress.

Focus can mean a practical set of steps to take. At the same time it can be the grand inspiration that guides your life and brings purpose to your actions. Every day focus can mean simply getting out of bed and doing what you need to do.

There are three types of focus that are critical to your success. The first is goal setting. This process is critical because everything else follows from it. After all, you can't make progress toward your goals until you have them.

> Consistency in practice will make it all happen.

Everyone should write down a set of short-term goals, intermediate goals, and long-term goals. In some sense, the long-term goals are the easiest. After all, if you're going to change careers, write the great American novel, and get a graduate degree, no one expects it to be done tomorrow. So it's easy to state the long-term goal because you don't have to do anything about it immediately.

Intermediate goals are a little tougher. Let's say your long-term goal is to change careers. What are the steps you need to take and what is the time frame? You need to write down the milestones: When will you start retraining? When will you get the certification?

Intermediate goals do two things for you: 1) They help you divide "the goal" into manageable, practical, smaller goals; and 2) They help you focus on the reality of getting from "here" to "there." What things need to be done? What's a realistic time frame?

Finally, the short-term goals help guide you today. Will you study an hour each day? Three hours a week? Pass the test by next Saturday?

Here you see that goal-setting helps you to focus specific activities. Here's what I'm doing today to reach my goals. Here's what I'm doing this week, this month, this quarter, this year. You can hold yourself accountable. If you tell someone else, they can hold you accountable.

Write down your goals!

Review your goals!

Share your Goals!

So, the first type of focusing on your success is goal-setting.

The second type of focus that is critical to your success is *working the plan*. You've heard the old saying "Plan the work and work the plan." You now have a series of goals – things that need to be done for you to reach the ultimate goal. You have plans that translate into actions for the year, month, week, and day.

Working the Plan means you get up every day and do what needs to be done to advance your goals. It might mean studying, reading, writing, preparing for a test, taking an exam.

Don't forget that your plan should include eating right and exercising so you can stay healthy. It should also include time to think. Perhaps meditation or prayer: Some quiet time to relax and put things in perspective. Remember, without relaxation there is no success!

And, of course, working the plan means focusing on those short-term goals and doing occasional checks on progress toward the intermediate and longer-term goals.

When I talk to people who are successful, I hear the same advice over and over again:

Get up every day. Do your work. Do your best. Get up the next day and do it again. Pretty soon you'll look back and find that you've made progress toward your goals.

I have a reminder on my calendar that is set to go off every morning at 6:00 AM. It simply says "RFS." To me that obviously means Relax Focus Succeed. More specifically, it means stop whatever I'm doing and go do one of the following items that contribute to my ultimate success:

- Exercise

- Quiet Reading

- Writing

- Meditation or Prayer

When I'm in the groove and working the plan, I'm already exercising or meditating when that alert goes off. It's only there so that, if I'm *not* working the plan, I've got a reminder to get back on track.

Note that these are not "work" activities. The list does not include filing paperwork, creating invoices, faxing quotes, making travel plans, doing payroll, etc.

The morning activities include things I need to be well-rounded, to keep my life in balance, and to allow me to make progress on the ultimate goals.

Part of working the plan is to remember the big picture.

You should not have a bifurcation between your professional life and your personal life. Your life is your life! Part of focusing on success is bringing harmony to these pieces of your one life. That's why you need a little time off for exercise and relaxation.

So let's go back to goal-setting for a minute. After you become comfortable with a few goals (don't overdo it at first), you may want to set goals for the three major areas of your life:

Personal (individual)

Family

Professional.

You may see some conflicts between these. In fact, if you don't see conflicts, you're probably in denial. We all have to balance different elements in our lives. Sometimes you feel guilty because you have to go to work when you should be spending time with the family. Sometimes you feel guilty because you have to spend time with the family and you can't put in the extra effort that's needed at work!

This balancing act never stops. No one ever gets it "right" for more than a week at a time.

Which brings us to the third type of focus you need for your success: evaluating your actions in light of your goals. Most people don't think of this as "focus" right away. But it may be the most important type of focus there is!

On a grand scale, you might ask yourself "If I make this decision, is it consistent with my overall goals?" But life is seldom so dramatic. It is actually easier to make big decisions and big purchases that are consistent with the "big picture."

More important are the hundreds of little decisions we make every day. Evaluating your actions in terms of your goals has to be more of a mindset and less of a calculation. It takes a special kind of focus. The answer has to be consistent with your goals and your values and your overall sense of how you want the world to operate.

Do you see why this is difficult? You have to know what your goals are and how they will have an impact on your daily life. You have to know your values. You have to have a sense of how you want the world to operate!

And this guiding perspective that unifies your personal life, your family life, and your professional life does not exist until you create it!

Young businesses (and young business people) are rarely successful unless they have commitment to guiding principles that helps them to make decisions. They need to have some way of translating "the big picture" into daily activities.

On a personal level that means taking time to relax and think (focus) about these issues at a time set aside so that you're not working, you're not getting the kids off to school, you're not paying the bills, etc.

The big picture doesn't create itself: You have to relax and you have to focus and you have to create it slowly over time.

Ths final type of focus–evaluating your actions in light of your goals–takes a long time to achieve. It relies on a great deal of work and thought.

When we say that a person "has focus" or "is a focused individual" we usually mean someone who has achieved this higher level. A focused person sees more opportunities than the rest of us because that person interprets almost everything in light of a specific world view.

A focused person reaches his goals sooner because more of his activities are related to those goals. It's not that he's a "calculating" person; it's that he has a big picture and most people don't. Having a big picture is one more tool he uses when making decisions.

A focused person has a high level of consistency between her work life, personal life, family life, spiritual life, and every other aspect of her life. There's a lot less switching hats between "Now I'm the boss; Now I'm the sister; Now I'm the environmentalist; Now I'm the entrepreneur." Consistency, by definition, means less fragmentation of the various roles you play in your life.

As a side benefit, this consistency also reduces stress.

Building Blocks of Success

Recall the discussion from Chapter Four on building a foundation of values and working up to daily activities that are built on those values. Building your success is very much like building a physical structure. This is true for individuals and families as much as it is for businesses.

ACTIVITIES
ROLES YOU PLAY
MISSION/VISION
PRINCIPLES/VALUES

You start with the foundation stones. They're big, hard to lift, difficult to place just where you want them. These foundation stones are your values and principles.

Just above the foundation are some slightly smaller stones. Still large, still difficult to place, but a little easier to manipulate because you have the foundation in place. This is your mission or your vision. This is where commitment starts. Everything above this is tied to behavior. Everything below is tied to belief.

Have you ever seen a construction project that got started and then stopped? Perhaps they ran out of materials. Perhaps they ran out of money, inspiration, dedication, drive, or desire. No matter why they stopped, it's a sad sight to see a project abandoned at the foundation stage.

I've heard it said that you have to have three catastrophic failures before you succeed. I don't buy that, but we do need to have some experience with failure. Perhaps this failure – catastrophic or not – is your abandoned foundation.

When the time comes to build *the right* foundation, a little experience helps. The foundation stones are just as heavy and just as hard to place. But maybe there's a better sense of what goes together and how to place the stones.

Once the foundation of your success is in place, you can continue building with somewhat smaller stones. These are the base of the walls. Again, you have some lessons to learn about choosing and placing stones.

Starting over at this level, above a well-built foundation, is no fun. But it's a lot better than building a new foundation! And so it goes, with each layer of bricks a little easier to place.

If you've done the hard work of building a solid foundation, with values and principles that truly represent who you are and what you believe, then building everything above that is a lot easier.

Most people never explore their foundation. They literally don't know what they stand for. They don't know what's more important and what's less important in their lives.

These lost souls have some vague idea about what's important and what's meaningful. But they don't have a rock solid foundation. So everything they've built is very shaky.

There's an old saying: You have to stand for something or you'll fall for anything. This is very true.

You get to rebuild your life, your belief systems, and your "foundation" every day, every week, every month. You can start over anytime you want, and become the person you want to be.

But once you've built a strong foundation, everything gets easier.

When you go to rebuild "from the ground up," you'll discover that you're not rebuilding that foundation at all. In fact, after you've taken about three serious attempts at it, you'll discover that you don't need to rebuild the foundation at all. In fact, you merely reaffirm the foundation and go to work on the roles and behavior.

And, even more than that, you'll discover that the higher layers need less adjustment as time goes on. As you work to build and re-affirm goals and your roles and your behavior, you will find more consistency over time.

Working on yourself is just like working on anything else: it becomes easier over time. Every time you go to work on yourself, you will have more techniques for success, you'll avoid more missteps, and the work will be faster, easier, and less painful.

Full Stop. Reboot.

Perhaps you're ready to say that, somewhere along the line, this became overwhelming. "Where do I begin?"

Begin small. Your success is not a sprint; it's a series of marathons. Don't try to run 26 miles the first day. Set a few simple goals. Set aside time every day to think and read and write about what you want to do. I promise that if you use that time every day, your goals will evolve. And consistency in practice will make it all happen.

What's the Style of Your Goals?

Setting goals is a great first step to success. In fact, it's a necessary first step. Once your goals are set, you can begin moving toward them. But what's the very next step? The very next step is to determine what kind of goals you have. Because the style of your goals will help you determine the approach you need to reach them.

Sequential Goals. Some goals have a definite series of steps that lead to a concluding state you can call "success." For example, building a chair, refurbishing an old car, or documenting the procedures in your department all fall into this category.

The job can be broken down into a distinct list of actions that lead up to a finished "product." These actions can include some rather large steps, such as "Get a Bachelor's Degree." Such large steps would themselves be divided into smaller, manageable steps.

With sequential goals, you can always work on the next step, always advance toward the ultimate goal. Some day the room will be painted, the loan will be paid off, the office manuals will be updated.

> How many goals can you do justice to at once?

On very large goals – ones that take years to complete and have several large steps within them – you may need to develop different resources and skill sets as you progress toward your ultimate goal. People often use the analogy of going down a long and winding road on the way to a goal. Sometimes, you need to take a "side trip" to learn a skill, earn some money, or otherwise prepare yourself for the next step.

Behavioral Goals. The other major type of goals are behavioral. They involve changes in habits. Most health related goals are behavioral in nature. There is no point at which you declare yourself healthy, sell your gym shorts, and never exercise again. Health involves a complex series of habits that you develop over time.

With all behavioral goals there is occasional back-sliding. Holidays, accidents, and a backlog of work can cause you to put off exercising for a month. After that, you're out of the habit of exercising. Now you need to re-gain those healthy habits and begin exercising again.

And, as you've probably guessed, many goals involve a combination of these attributes. If one of the steps to your ultimate goal is to get a degree, then developing good study habits will help you reach that goal. To write a novel, you need only write one or two pages a day (I'm told). The habit of sitting down every day to write will get you there.

And sequential goals can also help you to reach behavioral goals. After all, no one runs 10K the first day. You run half a mile and walk half a mile. You work up to running one mile, two miles, etc.

All success consists of the proper combination of habits, knowledge, and tools (see the introduction to Chapter Three).

So when you sit down and begin to work on your goals, remember that the first step is to determine the type or style of goal you have. Begin dissecting your goals and determine whether they are essentially sequential or behavioral. If your goals are sequential, plot out the steps you will take to fulfill your goals. Some steps will require

> "If you don't know what you want, how will you know when you get it? For that matter, how do you know you don't already have it?."
> – Keith Ellis

new habits (behaviors). If your goals are behavioral, develop a plan for acquiring the habits (and discipline) you need to fulfill your goals.

Revise your plan from time to time. Not too often. But often enough so that you remind yourself of where you're going and how you plan to get there. If you've broken your goals into smaller, more manageable pieces, you should see progress – both sequential and behavioral.

The more fully you examine your goals, the fresher they become in your mind. And the more details you give them, the more real they become for you.

Dissecting your goals and categorizing the "parts" will make your goals easier to reach and less overwhelming. Try it today!

> "To allow oneself to be carried away by a multitude of conflicting concerns, to surrender to too many demands, to commit oneself to too many good projects, to want to help everyone and everything, is itself to succumb to the violence of our time."
> – Thomas Merton

Summary and Conclusions

Just as in the last chapter, all of this work is very delicate and serious. After all, we're building a new YOU. So we're in dangerous territory. You need to take it seriously

Let me also assure you that you don't have to change who you are. At the very most basic level, we all have things we are and things we aren't. We all have things we like and things we don't. The goal here is not to change who you are, but to help you see who you are, and to build a foundation for your success that's based in who you really are.

There's tremendous stress when people try to live someone else's dream, or when they try to accept someone else's values.

I'm not kidding when I say that this is dangerous territory.

If you proceed to build a vision, roles, and daily activities that are all based on values and principles that are not your own, you are headed for disaster. Your foundation – your values and principles – must be your own.

People who have personal crises and emotional breakdowns frequently use the terminology that they are living someone else's life. They're pursuing someone else's goals. They're fulfilling someone else's dream.

You can't do that. Or at least you can't do it forever.

You're much better off starting over with nothing and following your own dream than to continue on a stressful path of following a dream that's not your own.

One of the saddest and most powerful experiences of my life happened when I first started teaching college. I was in my second year of graduate school at the University of Michigan, and it was my first year as a teaching assistant.

Very early on, in the first week of class, two female students came to visit me. They had some trumped up excuse to drop by my office and ask about the class. My impression as they left was that they were both "A" students. They were strangers until two weeks before. Now they were two friends starting out their college careers.

When I think back to my own undergraduate experience, it was fun and difficult and exciting. And so I assumed it was for these two.

A week later, however, one of the two women came into my office terribly upset. Her friend had committed suicide. She was, in fact, a straight A student who had always excelled at everything she did. And in another environment she would have been very successful.

But in this environment, with forty thousand students, all of whom were in the top 5% of their high school class, she was overwhelmed. She felt pressure from her parents to succeed. In fact, she felt so much pressure that she didn't feel like she could go back home and say "Can I please just quit?"

Even today, more than twenty years later, it makes me very sad to think about her. I pray that I will never feel that kind of pressure, that I will never put that kind of pressure on another person, and that my daughter will never feel that she can't come to me and say "Daddy, please help me out."

As you can see, I take this work very seriously.

Most people will never go so far down the path of following someone else's dream that they will feel so trapped that suicide is the only way out. But there *are* many people who are unhappy (and miserable, really) because they're not following their own dreams.

You deserve to have a happy, healthy, balanced, and fulfilling life. That life comes from having consistency between your principles, your vision, and the activities of your daily life. When there's consistency between the roles you play at work and at home, then there's personal happiness. When there's consistency between the roles you play in the community and in your personal life, then there's personal fulfillment.

That's why we work on it every day. That's why this work takes precedence over every other thing.

If you do this goal-setting and soul-searching, it will dra-
matically improve every aspect of your life.

To Ponder

"Authentic values are those by which
a life can be lived, which can form a
people that produces great deeds and
thoughts."

— Allan Bloom

"Forgetting   your   mission   leads,
inevitably, to getting tangled up in
details — details that can take you
completely off your path."

— Laurie Beth Jones

"Oh, it's delightful to have ambitions.
I'm so glad I have such a lot. And there
never seems to be any end to them —
that's the best of it. Just as soon as you
attain to one ambition you see another
one glittering higher up still. It does
make life so interesting."

— Anne of Green Gables
by L.M. Montgomery

Chapter 9

Exercise, Physical Activity, and Balance

Introduction:
I Have Every Excuse Not to Exercise

Some mornings I get up and would rather stay in bed. I'm sure this is unique to me. ☺

I know I need to exercise, but reading is more fun. And I have bills to pay. And my back hurts. Also, I need to tidy up my office, the cat needs feeding, I should really take it easy on that injured foot, I think I'm getting a headache, and I just don't feel like it.

We all have excuses for not doing exercise. The more people I meet, the more excuses I see. But I've noticed something: The people who do exercise regularly have just as many reasons not to exercise as the people who don't exercise regularly. In fact, people who exercise regularly seem always to be discussing how their shoulder aches or that knee surgery slowed them down. They have shin splints and bad backs and various maladies that could be used as an excuse to avoid exercise.

But these people also have something else: A sense of why they should exercise.

Exercise is one of the most fundamental elements of success. No matter how you define success, you will need a working physical body to achieve it. You can certainly get rich and be fat. But success doesn't mean getting rich. Success means attaining your goals. That means you need some balance in your life (you have to focus enough to know what your goals are and to move toward them).

And to enjoy your success, you need a body that works. One of my favorite modern philosophers is Dr. Dean Edell (see Healthcentral.com). I call him a philosopher because he has a consistent, moderate, rational approach to health. He likes to put in perspective the news we hear about living longer. If we can extend the life expectancy of Americans by some period of time, he says, we need to consider the quality of that life extension. Are we living another three months in a hospital, hooked up to equipment that keeps us alive? If so, is there value in extending life expectancy?

Wouldn't it be great if you could extend your life and know that you'll be upright, active, and reasonably healthy for that extended period of time?

At the turn of the millennium, I told my daughter Victoria (then age 8) that she had a real chance of seeing and remembering three centuries – the 1900's, the 2000's, and the 2100's. All she had to do was live to be 108. If you think about the advancements in medicine, being 108 years old in the year 2100 seems quite reasonable.

Then she asked me if people might live to be 140 by that time. I told her I thought they could. At least some people will live to be 140 years old. So she told me that I could also see the year 2100 if I worked at it and took care of myself. So, now I have to exercise for two reasons: She's going to be mad at me if I don't live to 140, and I want to be ambulatory and able to enjoy it!

You may not have a goal of living to be 140, but you should have the goal of being healthy while you're here on earth. Heart attacks, strokes, cancer: All of these make life less enjoyable and more of a challenge. But exercise can help keep all of them away.

You're excuses are worthless. There are people with all kinds of maladies who exercise regularly. If you're reasonably able, you need to exercise more than them.

Some people use the excuse that exercise is expensive, but you don't have to spend any money at all. There's an old fellow in my neighborhood who jogs in basic khaki shorts and a button-up shirt. He doesn't even spend the money for a pair of exercise shorts! But he jogs many miles every day. He looks like he's in his sixties, but he's probably in his eighties. He won't even spend $15 on a t-shirt, but he exercises regularly.

Exercise is pretty straight-forward: Move your body more and you'll live longer.

I'm no Charles Atlas. In fact, if you met me on the street you'd probably never guess that I exercise at all. But I ride the exercycle, I do yoga, and I walk. Because of my arthritis, I sometimes walk with a cane. But I walk. I have lots of excuses why I can't run or play racquetball anymore. But I can do something, and I try.

When I travel (which is often), I try to stay in a hotel with exercise facilities. In fact, I'm one of the few people who travel with both a fold-up cane and exercise clothes. I don't normally need the cane, but long plane rides and convention center chairs can take their toll.

If you have to boil success down to a few basic elements, exercise has to be on the short list. If you reach your goals and find yourself bedridden (or dead), then you haven't really achieved anything at all. You have to take care of your frail human shell because you'll need it to be in good shape no matter what you achieve.

Now we're going to start with one of the easiest exercises of all: breathing.

Relaxation Breathing

Here's a basic outline for a simple relaxation breathing exercise. As with everything else, the basic technique is simple – It's the daily effort to practice that's difficult.

> If you know how to relax, you will stay focused.

(Note: If you're interested in a spoken guide to this exercise, you may download one for free from the RelaxFocusSucceed.com web site.)

The major part of this relaxation technique involves breathing. Here's what you do:

Sit comfortably with your legs uncrossed.
Your hands should be open.
Your eyes should be closed.

Take a deep breath. If you wish, count silently
as you breath in.
One Two Three Four Five.
Hold it for a five count and then let it out.
One Two Three Four Five.
Again.

Breath in through your nose.
Breath out through your mouth.
And again.
In Two Three Four Five.
Pause.
Out Two Three Four Five.

Now breath normally.
As you breath in, focus your attention on one
specific part of your body. Keep your attention
there as you breath out.
Let your attention move from your head to your
neck, to your shoulders and your back.
Now to your elbows, wrists, and fingers.
To your hips and then your knees.
To your ankles, feet, and toes.
Take time at each "stop."

If noises interfere, make note of them, but do not let them grab your attention. Simply bring your focus back to your breathing.

When you're finished, slowly bring yourself back to full awareness. Think about being ten layers deep in meditation.

Count one, two. Becoming a little more aware.
Count three four. Take a deep breath.
Count five six. Wiggle your toes. Stretch your hands.
Count seven eight. You're almost alert. Take another breath.
Count nine ten. Slowly open your eyes.
Sit for a minute and relax. Make sure you're completely awake before you stir.

You can see that this is much easier to get started if you have someone guiding you through it.

This basic technique is surprisingly relaxing and refreshing. It is also quite enjoyable.

If you're like me, you might experience some pains when you do this exercise. We automatically block a certain amount of physical, mental, and emotional pain just so we can get through the day.

But there is a difference between pain and suffering. Pain tells us information we need to know. We often change our behavior to reduce pain. We adjust our exercise routine, or how we lift something, or the way we work. This is good.

But fear of pain can keep us from doing things we should do. Focusing on the pain can help us to understand how much we should be adjusting our behavior. Sometimes the pain is simply a minor irritation and we should work through it. At other times the pain is limiting and we need to back off and respect it.

In addition to the physical pain, our mind also blocks some types of mental or emotional pain. We lessen the pain by altering our memories, numbing our reactions, and literally "blocking out" certain painful events. Breathing techniques can help people to understand the pain and learn to live with it.

I was surprised at how some simple breathing techniques can help in dealing with pain.

I began doing breathing/relaxing exercises regularly. I even set an alarm so I don't get carried away or fall asleep.

Explore a bit. You'll find several types of relaxation techniques. These include praying, meditation, journal writing, other writing, and reading contemplative books.

Breathing should be the basis of all "quiet time." There are many ways to relax and let your body rejuvenate. They should all start by getting comfortable and taking some deep cleansing breaths.

The Next Step

Eventually, the ability to relax will become "portable." A few breaths under any circumstances and your body will relax – because it knows the routine.

The physiology of relaxation breathing is quite amazing. You lower your pulse and blood pressure – instantly. I have a heart rate monitor that I use while exercising. While riding my exercise bicycle one day I decided to measure my ability to reduce my heart rate.

After warming up and getting deep in the aerobic zone – a pulse of 140 – I tried it. While maintaining the same pace I closed my eyes and took three cleansing breaths. I was able to drop my pulse by 12 points instantly!

Now I play a game at the doctor's office. You know how they take your blood pressure even if you come in for a stubbed toe? I decided to try my relaxation exercises there. It works like a charm. I always ask how I did and the nurses usually comment that my blood pressure is "very good." I can usually bring it to 100/50.

In addition to permanently lowering your blood pressure, relaxation breathing has other benefits.

In any stressful situation, a few breaths will calm you and help you focus on what's important. Try it when you go into a performance review, a job interview, or a meeting with a difficult person. Take a few deep cleansing breaths and relax. It won't make you perfectly relaxed, but it will help.

In many situations you don't want to be perfectly relaxed – you want to keep your edge. But a few deep breaths can take you one step toward relaxation and increase your focus. You can gain an edge by viewing the situation at a slightly slower pace and viewing things as they really are.

With adrenaline coursing through your body, you can become a bit more focused, but also more agitated. Breathing techniques help you to step back from the edge, maintain control, and focus your mind more accurately on your objectives.

There's an old adage that the first one to lose his temper also loses the argument (or fight or negotiation). Breathing properly gives you the power to stay focused and not lose your temper.

We all have experiences we wish we could live over. "I wish I hadn't lost my temper." Or cried, or stormed out, or used those words.

We know we need to focus on doing the right thing. We need to not get carried away by the emotions and stress of the moment. That's what we want. That's what we need to succeed.

Very often we see examples of "greatness" in which the hero is the person who "had the presence of mind" to do the right thing. Or it was the person who "kept her wits about her" when everyone else panicked.

Relaxation does not mean going to sleep. It can be a simple step back from the edge of stress, or panic, or overwhelming emotions. Relaxation brings focus. It brings control and rationality and a constant awareness of why we are engaged in a specific activity. It keeps us pointed toward our goals and keeps things in perspective.

We need that adrenaline. And the stress. They push us and motivate us and give us strength we might not otherwise have. But they can also kill us. Relaxation breathing brings focus. It gives us the power to turn every action, every meeting, every event to our advantage. With focus you can turn everything you do into a piece of the puzzle that will be your success. Focus and every action you take will be a step toward your own success.

Channel your energy and other people's energy toward your success. If you stay focused, you will have success. If you know how to relax you will stay focused.

And hence . . .

> Relax
>
>> Focus
>>
>>> Succeed®

Mind-Body Connections

We are constantly learning new things about the connection between our mind and our physical body. This connection seems almost obvious to us in the twenty-first century. But it hasn't always been so clear. And even today we see a never-ending series of research reports that verify the relationship.

Among other things, we see reports like this:

- Laughter can reduce pain, stress, and inflammation. It is also known to speed healing after an injury and provide a world of other benefits.

- Patience is related to high blood pressure. Or, I should say, impatience is correlated with high blood pressure.

- Vacations are correlated with longer life! People who take regular vacations can lower their death rates by 20-50%.

- Taking naps during the day at work can help you clear your head, make fewer mistakes, improve your memory, and make you a more pleasant person to be around.

- Procrastination is correlated with having trouble sleeping and minor health issues such as the common cold.

- Meditation lowers blood pressure and leads to higher levels of concentration, better sleep, and less stress.

- Exercise in general is good for your heart, your weight, your blood pressure, your sleep pattern, your bone density, and a very long list of other benefits.

- Contentment lowers levels of the stress hormone cortisol and a protein called plasma fibrinogen. Cortisol leads to inflammation (which leads to pain). Plasma fibrinogen protein leads to heart disease.

- Yoga has been shown to reduce stress, reduce pain, increase concentration, and even help you lose weight.

- Writing – such as a journal – can reduce stress levels. It is also a great way to help focus your attention on things that matter.

- Prayer can help you stay healthy. Interestingly, research even shows that intercessory prayer (when one person prays for another) can reduce pain and inflammation in the "recipient."

- Hobbies reduce stress, increase contentment, and improve positive mental attitude generally.

- And More!

If you keep your eyes open for these types of connections, you'll find them all over the place. Many of these "common sense" connections have been the focus of intense research over the last thirty years.

The best news is that these behaviors can be learned. Whether you naturally laugh a lot or you need to "teach" yourself to laugh more, you get the benefits associated with the behavior.

For some things, this makes obvious sense. After all, if you exercise, you expect the benefits of exercise, and if you take naps you expect the benefits of taking naps. But it is less obvious that some of these behaviors will bring the benefits listed above. Still, it's true.

Contentment, for example, is related to positive mental attitude, time pressures, and stress. When you're mentally or physically stressed, all your emotions conspire to bring down your positive energy. And that depletes your physical energy, which means you're less likely to spring into an exercise routine or other activities that can bring you back "up."

Research has shown, for many of these behaviors, that you can actually force the positive benefits upon yourself. If you don't naturally laugh a lot, for example, you can adjust your television exposure to include more stupid sit-coms and less news. This will improve your attitude – whether you like it or not!

Some things are harder to work on than others. Overcoming procrastination, for example, is partly a behavior you can change and partly tied in with other issues. For most people, procrastination is related to time pressures, which means stress. It often means that there are too many things on your "to do" list, and you know you won't get them all done.

That situation leads to less exercise, no naps, no vacations, no hobbies, etc. (you don't have the time). It doesn't take much energy to see that these are all related. In a balanced life

> Making a commitment to a new way of life is not simply whispering in exhaustion that something has to change.

you have work and play, time on and time off, exercise, hobbies, writing, prayers – and the occasional nap.

In other words, balance can bring you all the health benefits listed above.

But how do you get started?

That's up to you. First, make the commitment that it's what you want.

Making a commitment to a new life means accepting in your heart and mind that everything has to change, and deciding that you will do the hard work necessary to make it happen.

Second, pick a place to start and then begin. Start with laughter or meditation or exercise. Or start with a hobby and writing and a nap. It doesn't matter. This is a whole new you and you have the rest of your life to make improvements.

Third, design a plan to add each of these elements to your life. Little by little everything will get better. And that will make each step a little easier.

Improve everything in your life! What a great goal. Let's get started today!

Working Toward Balance

Balance in anything is difficult to achieve and maintain. This is true in your job, in your family, and with friends. It's true of finances and values and priorities.

One of the great benefits of collecting and re-reading books on your business and your success is that the project of being successful is never done. Whether you're working on success with your business, in a hobby, or your relationship with your spouse, the job is never done.

> "Inertia is the single greatest barrier to success. It's also the easiest to overcome. All you have to do is act."
> – Keith Ellis

Many years ago there was a saying that appeared on T-shirts and posters: "Be patient: God isn't finished with me yet." This is true of all of us. We are all works in progress.

I encourage you to bring balance to this work in progress. That means work a little on this and a little on that. When we focus too much on one aspect of our development, we neglect the other aspects. This is perhaps the reason we're never "done."

Like many others, I went through a phase when I focused very strongly on establishing myself in my field. I logged into the work computer from home at 5 AM, worked twelve hour days, and was always available when work demanded it. As you might imagine, my wife was not happy about this and we had to work out an agreement on our priorities. As soon as I looked at the situation, of course, I saw what I had done and realized that I wasn't happy living like that.

I vowed to balance my personal life with my work. Now it is rare for me to work late or work on the weekends. And when I do, my wife is completely understanding and supportive. That's part of the balance.

As fate would have it, I moved from the job of tremendous unbalance to a contract position with Hewlett Packard, the great computer company. The particular unit in which I worked had a mission statement that included a belief in balancing work with life.

This mission statement – that we value the balance between work and life – was printed on their memos, their stationary, on overheads, slides, handbooks, etc. It was everywhere. Subtle and small print. A true "background" message. And in all the small subtle ways you can imagine, this sense of balance filled the atmosphere. It wasn't perfect. There was hard work and stress. But the ethic of balance was always present and this made the work a lot less stressful.

In my own business I find that my feeble human mind can only focus on one thing at a time. So the project of the moment might be education or writing or doing the work of my clients. And when I find that I am too absorbed by one thing, other things suffer.

At one point I decided to push the "quality" aspect of my practice. I spent time fine-tuning my mission statement and writing memos to clients on what they could expect from my company. I focused on our organization and philosophy and commitment to quality. I created a series of "promises" to send to my clients and prospects so they could see what a great company we were.

All of this was valuable work, but in short order I realized that I had gotten carried away with all this quality stuff. I had dedicated so much time to the development of a quality ethic that I had fallen behind on my promises for some deadlines and I had a stack of job proposals that needed to get out.

In my business, I need to get proposals out to clients so they can say "yes," so I can work! In this case, I got carried away with focusing on something that is good for my business but it ended up hurting my business in the long run. Now I schedule time for "development" activities.

Balance is a simple concept and we somehow think it is easy to achieve. In fact, balance is extremely difficult – if not impossible – to achieve. This is true in part because it is a moving target.

All lives are filled with change. So after much work you feel that you are approaching balance. That's when God throws you a curve ball. Most people have to balance schedules for themselves, their spouses, their children, school, church, customers, and so forth. And everyone's life just keeps on changing.

So you see, moving toward balance is a never-ending chore. And it's okay if you never reach it because that would mean your world stopped changing long enough for you to catch up. Wouldn't that be boring?

The most difficult thing about achieving balance in your life is to realize that your goal is moving and your job is never done. Once you accept this, the process of achieving balance can reduce stress in your life.

Once you get close to being "in balance" you will find it easy to make adjustments in your life in order to maintain balance.

It is much more difficult to achieve balance than it is to maintain balance. Once you achieve balance (to the extent that's possible), mid-course corrections are easy.

Humans have a very strong resistance to change. We are comfortable in our habits. As a result, we resist change and we even deny that change is happening. Mentally, we want to stay with the comfortable "present" and don't accept the fact that our vision of the present has already become the past.

Sometimes our lives are slow and maintaining balance is like keeping your car on the road during a leisurely drive in the country. At other times changes come so fast that you feel like you're stuck inside a video game with fifty things going on at once and it takes everything you have to stay in the game, let alone balance in the middle.

The process of getting comfortable with change and balance is difficult. It may help to think of balance as a goal unto itself. You can develop the habit of maintaining balance. When uncomfortable change comes, you can retreat to your habit of maintaining balance rather than retreating to old behaviors that resist the inevitable change.

None of this is meant to suggest that you should accept all changes and merely react to the world, bouncing around with no control over your life. Quite the opposite is true. Once you know and accept that change is coming, you can prepare for it. More than that, you can influence it, shape it, mold it, and make the future your own.

Every change represents an opportunity to mold the future. Most people react to change. They do not actively partici-pate in the creation of their own future! Practicing balance puts you in control of your own life.

Summary and Conclusions

I realize this is an odd chapter. We started with relaxation breathing and ended with a discussion of balance. I hope you can see the progression.

> If everything's top priority, then nothing's top priority.

In some sense, balance allows you to slow down. I like to tell people that it's your secret super power. When you have a vision about how the world should operate, and you can use a couple of deep breaths to put things in perspective, you can always be a little calmer and a little more in control.

Some people rush around trying to make everything they need an emergency. But, as I've learned running a service business, you can't make everything first priority.

Physical exercise of any kind helps us maintain balance. Breathing exercises help us maintain that balance and make it portable.

I've always considered exercise to be an important part of the "relax" component in Relax Focus Succeed®. If nothing else, it can wear you out and help you sleep! And there are plenty of benefits in that.

To Ponder

"The reason we all need a personal philosophy and goals is so we will have them to rely on in times of stress."
— Karl W. Palachuk

"There is nothing more galling to angry people than the coolness of those on whom they wish to vent their spleen."
— Alexandre Dumas

"Success is a journey – not a destination."
— H. Tom Collard

Section IV:

Behavior and Habits

Perhaps it's all my education in Political Science, Sociology, and social research, but I am a behavioralist. It's not that I don't care how people think, but people's thoughts don't affect me until they become actions – behaviors.

You can have all the successful thoughts and intentions in the world. But successful intentions plus four hours on the couch watching reruns will not make you successful.

On the Relax Focus Success® web site, you'll find lots of quotations likes these:

"Form good habits and become their slave."
– Og Mandino

"Habit and routine have an unbelievable power to waste and destroy."
– Henri de Lubac

"Habit is a cable; we weave a thread of it each day, and at last we cannot break it."

– Horace Mann

"The victory of success is half won when one gains the habit of work."

– Sarah Bolton

Most of us have a vision of ourselves based, in large part, by our habits. So, to the extent that we wish to change who we are, we need to address both the vision and the habits. The habits color the vision. The vision drives the habits. But the habit drive themselves as well.

Very often, we have to stop doing things in order to be successful. Because stopping bad habits is the only way to make room for good habits.

In this section we look at a combination who you are, who you want to become, and the habits that will get you from here to there. We also formally introduce two concepts that have been working throughout the book.

In Chapter Ten we look at reforming yourself and moving to the next version of yourself. We revisit the discussion of You and You2 from Chapter Seven. In Chapter Eleven we address the concept of consciously forming habits that will drive your success.

Chapter 10

Who You Are and Who You Will Be

Introduction: Accept Reality

It seems odd to tell people to "Accept Reality," but many people have trouble with this. Just because you accept reality doesn't mean you're giving up on making it better.

There are many things we don't want to accept in our personal lives and at work.

- You can't please everyone.
- You will make mistakes.
- Others will make mistakes.
- Things break.
- Sometimes people disappoint you (and you them).
- Sometimes you don't reach your goals.

and so forth.

Like many people, your reaction to this list may be "That all sounds pessimistic. I need to have a positive attitude." Yes, it sounds pessimistic, but it's not. And, yes, you need to have a positive attitude. But ignoring reality won't help you a bit. Let's take disappointment for example.

> Accept reality and turn that acceptance into a positive philosophy that makes you a better person.

Some people believe that accepting the fact that you will disappoint someone means you've given up or you no longer need to try your best. This isn't true at all. You are very likely to disappoint someone today. And I guarantee you will disappoint someone in the next week. Some of it's your fault and some of it's theirs.

You might over-promise (in an attempt to not disappoint), or be the victim of circumstances or an urgent interruption. Others might want you to volunteer and be disappointed by your silence. Or they'll expect you to do something you did before even though they never asked.

As a successful person, you want others to have high expectations of you. You encourage this with acts and words. Some expectations are set by you and some are set by others and their assumptions of how you will act.

So you don't join a committee, you miss one phone call, or you're late for a meeting. Whatever it is, you have disappointed someone. Accepting the reality of this situation will help you reduce stress, deal with the situation, and be a better person.

Sometimes we need to be attentive to the times when we disappoint others. Take the opportunity to talk about it and "adjust" future expectations. Evaluate your own failings and adopt procedures to set more realistic deadlines.

The point is, you can develop a philosophy to deal with disappointment. It doesn't mean you "put up with" or encourage it. Disappointment is a reality and you make something positive out of it by developing your attitude or response before it happens. The same is true when people disappoint you.

Developing your personal philosophy about responding to disappointments will reduce stress in your life and give you a sense of perspective that will help you to stay focused on success when disappointment happens.

Think about it. There's no longer a "need" to go ballistic, make someone feel guilty, get in their face, and add stress to the situation the next time you're disappointed. You can determine today that your response will be productive and positive and you'll take the time to think it out.

The same is true with mistakes and other "unforeseen" events. Some stuff just happens. Accepting the fact that you (and other people) will make mistakes allows you to develop a philosophy of response that reduces stress and focuses on learning and moving forward.

It doesn't mean you will put less effort into avoiding mistakes. It *does* mean you'll recover more quickly and learn something for next time.

I used to be in charge of data entry at a company that tracked all the activity of the state legislature. We had dozens of college students doing the data entry work. After I came on board and learned the job, I noticed that there was a lot of stress among the data entry people. They were very conscientious and concerned about making mistakes. I realized that part of this was due to the fact that we were using an arcane computer system and they were afraid of "breaking" it.

With computers there is a fear sometimes that you will "wipe out" hundreds of hours of work with the wrong keystroke. There is also frustration in learning because you can do something that causes you to lose your work and start over.

Anyway, I saw that people were working slower than they should because they were afraid to make mistakes. I took three actions to correct this. First, we developed a formal training for all the staff. Instead of a "sink or swim" approach, we showed them how all the data entry programs worked together. This gave the staff a sense of where their work fit in the big picture and a sense of confidence.

Second, I developed a formal policy about mistakes: Mistakes happen; fix them! We told the staff (quite honestly) that there is nothing they can "break" that we can't fix. All the data is backed up every night. In addition, the data entry logons simply don't have the power to destroy very much.

I spent a lot of time with the shift supervisors to make sure they understood the philosophy. If you make people feel bad about mistakes, they'll work too slowly and they may not report mistakes. We created an atmosphere in which people relaxed, worked faster, and reported their mistakes right away.

The third change was to implement some data checking reports that had fallen into disuse. These institutionalized a focus on accuracy and let everyone know that we worked every day to keep the data "clean."

The philosophical change to accept mistakes and build policies that acknowledge them resulted in faster data entry, fewer mistakes (because of training, self confidence and error checking), and a positive work environment. No one was ever afraid to tell a supervisor that they entered the wrong votes or deleted bill summaries.

The reaction to mistakes was totally, 100% focused on fixing the problem.

Although your first reaction to this philosophy might be that we have lowered our standards, that's not the case. In the three years after this philosophy was implemented, we had only one employee whose mistakes became an issue. And I assure you it was due to lazy, sloppy habits. That's not bad out of 50 poorly-paid data entry personnel over three years!

Accepting the reality that we make mistakes, or disappoint people, or don't reach our goals, does not have to be a pessimistic, defeatist statement. With some creativity we can accept reality and focus on how to fit this "fact" into our philosophy of success.

In the world of sports we accept that failures occur. It's not possible for a major league basketball team to be undefeated for the season. The best golfer in history can't win every tournament. We know this and accept this. It doesn't make us defeatist.

Accept reality and turn that acceptance into a positive philosophy that makes you a better person.

"Stuff" is Gonna Happen: Dealing with Mistakes

Decide now how you will react when problems happen.

We all make mistakes. We personally, our bosses, our employees, our loved ones. We all have problems.

I believe you can plan your reaction to unplanned events. Think about fires. We all have some idea of what to do in a fire. If you're not sure, ask a five-year old: Make sure doors and windows are closed. Feel doors for heat before you open them. Crawl out below the smoke. Go to the nearest exit. Meet in a safe place.

You don't have to go into as much detail, but you can prepare some elements of a response to any event.

On your job you can decide how to react to problems before they happen. If a computer fails, what will you do? How about if someone messes up the main database? And when coffee spills down the back of that expensive equipment and fries it?

Stuff Happens.

Sometimes our reaction is to yell and scream, wring our hands, and generally make the situation worse than it is. As you might imagine, I recommend against this approach. You can decide right now that the next problem will not be an instant crisis. When "stuff" happens, you can plan to take a deep breath and focus on the three stages of solving most problems:

- What can we do immediately to address this problem?

- How will we fix whatever went wrong?

- How can we avoid this in the future?

Here's an example: You are preparing a mailing of 5,000 pieces and the new employee somehow manages to break the folding machine. If this were 50 pieces it would be a minor inconvenience. Of course this happens at 5:05 PM on a Friday and the mailing has to be out in the Saturday mail.

Yelling, screaming, and firing people doesn't address the problem. Take a deep breath. The first stage is to solve the immediate problem and get the mailing folded. It's "only" 5:05 PM, so get someone to call printing houses and mailing houses. Perhaps you know another business with a folding machine. If all else fails, line up all the teenagers you can find for a 9:00 AM folding party.

Stage two involves fixing the problem. Leave an urgent message for the office repair company and try to get someone out first thing in the morning. You'll be amazed what some businesses are willing to do when you tell them it's a crisis. There are some great repair businesses out there. When you find one, make a point of using them again and tell your friends about the good experience.

Finally, stage three involves planning to avoid this problem in the future. Was the new employee trained properly and supervised? If so, what happened that could be avoided next time?

My general advice when people make mistakes is to use it as a learning experience and move on. Forgiveness should be instant and accompanied by learning.

If someone is excruciatingly incompetent, that's another story. But mistakes happen. There is never anything to be gained by yelling and screaming and firing people.

In *Don't Sweat the Small Stuff at Work*, Richard Carlson discusses forgiving yourself when you make mistakes. He notes that this does not mean that you have lower standards or use this as an excuse to slack off when it comes to quality. The same is true of forgiving others.

By planning a response beforehand, you can react to a "crisis" in a way that produces a positive atmosphere, addresses the problem quickly, and makes it "safe" for people to tell you when they make mistakes.

Yelling and screaming creates an atmosphere in which people are likely to cover up mistakes or walk away and not say anything (or spend good energy creating a good excuse).

And in the long run, we all look to certain people when problems occur because these people seem to keep their calm, generate ideas, and are generally "part of the solution." I hope such people are promoted and rewarded for their resourcefulness.

You can become one of these people. Decide now how you will react when problems happen. Unfortunately, "stuff" happens and you'll get a chance to test your new approach sooner or later.

Everything You Know May be Wrong

There's a great little bitty book entitled *The Elizabethan World Picture* by E.M.W. Tillyard. It summarizes the "knowledge" of science, religion, philosophy, and politics in the age of Queen Elizabeth.

This books is a great read for two reasons. First, it helps the modern thinker to understand what people believed and how those beliefs fit into the "common knowledge" of Sharespeare, Donne, Milton, Spenser, and others. Second, and perhaps more importantly, the book helps us to understand why newer, more modern explanations were rejected so completely when first introduced.

> Between "Reality" and your perception of reality, your perception is more important.
>
> Be prepared to re-think truths you have accepted.

How can the earth revolve around the sun when everyone knows that all the celestial bodies revolve around the earth?

It is possible that everything we know is wrong.

Stop: Think about that.

If the earth is spinning, then why do objects fall straight down? If I drop a rock from a high place, why does it not land some distance from where I dropped it?

The more scientific we become, the more arrogant we are about our knowledge. When I was a kid, in the 60's and 70's, "everyone" believed in the Big Bang Theory. Even in graduate school I remember hearing from a science major that the Big Bang was an undisputed truth. Now, in the early days of the 21st century, it isn't the truth anymore. In fact, we've already passed through a period in which it was hotly debated and now there are several schools of thought that reject the Big Bang and spend their energy debating alternative hypotheses.

The same may be true for your business and personal life. We all learn things because they make sense; they fit in with how we understand the world. They fit into our "world picture."

But so much of how we understand the world is a product of our social experience and our personal experience, that what we know might not be true at all. This is why leaders have to be open to new ideas and why managers need to listen to recommendations from new employees.

I can't tell you how many times I've heard someone say "We tried that" or "Our customers aren't interested in that." At some time in the past, the company tried something and it didn't work. So they now know it won't work. They know forever their customers aren't interested. They know you can't make money doing that.

In other words, the company is now unwilling to try things because their world view informs them that it won't work.

In the meantime, the world keeps spinning. Customers are ready for something today they weren't ready for a year ago. Customers have become more sophisticated and understand more than they did two years ago. Customers are tired of doing things the old way and wish someone would sell them a better solution.

Remember this: Your personal evolution takes place when your attitude is ready to receive a new message and the message is presented in a manner that aligns with your current attitude. That's why it's so important to keep reading material in your field.

You may read about a specific approach or concept ten times but it doesn't strike you as true or relevant. Then one day your attitude is just right: You're open to making some changes and you think you know the direction to head. When you're open to change and you read that same concept again, and it's worded just the right way, it suddenly sounds true and profound. Ten times it was just an interesting idea, but today it will change your business or your life.

The same is true for people as well as businesses. Do you *know* that someone will never accept the new policy? Do you *know* that someone will never leave the company? Do you *know* your spouse isn't willing to change?

What exactly do you know and why do you know it? Is what you know real? How are you limiting your success because you know something that stands in your way?

Be open.

Be open to the possibility that everything
you know is wrong.

Practical Example: Having Both Sides of the Conversation

One of the glories of being married is getting to know someone very well. One of the challenges of being married is the temptation to assume that, because you know this person so well, you know how she will respond to a request or an idea. I'm very guilty of this. I don't ask to do something I want to do because I know what the response will be. In other words, I have both sides of the conversation and never bother my wife with the need to provide her half.

And this is just silly. First, people change over time. Second, I am really assuming and not asking. Third, this is a very limiting behavior. Even if she says "no," she'll know that I'm interested.

We do this in our personal lives and at work. We don't ask for what we want (from bosses, from employees, from co-workers). We "know" what the answer is, so we don't ask. This is a huge, nation-wide, horrible problem. It reinforces inertia in the worst way. Not only do we resist change because we're comfortable, we also resist it because we assume we know how others will react. So continuing to do the same thing (even though everyone knows it's not as good as it could be) is easier than proposing changes.

Try this in your office: Agree to stop limiting your conversation – for one week – due to any assumptions about how someone will respond. Obviously you'll have some fun around this. Then notice that ideas come out and some real creative energy will emerge. In addition, those long-held "No we can't do that" policies may be re-evaluated!

It can't hurt and it might be great for revitalizing the business.

How are you limiting your success
because you *know* something that stands in your way?

You and You2
Who Will You Become?

Did you drift through the last five years?

I have been many people. We all have.

I recall fondly being a bare-foot boy spending summers at the park with my brothers. For a time, I was a college student immersed in intellectual endeavors. I enjoyed many years as a radio broadcaster and as a teacher. Somewhere along the line I became a husband and father and a nurturer.

These weren't roles or masks or facades. Each was "who I am."

I am sad sometimes when I look back on a former "me" and miss that person. I miss that guy who loved music so much that he listened to four or five albums a day, every day. I miss the graduate student who could blow a whole day talking political philosophy with my best friend Peter. I miss being a brand new father with the blessing every day of holding a baby girl no bigger than my arm. I miss the newly-married man with a loving bride and no children.

We all carry these former selves around with us. They're part of who we are.

And the most amazing thing is that – stop to think about this – these former selves were truly different people from our current selves. They had different motivations, different jobs, different friends, different hobbies, and different problems. They got up at a different time of day, had a different morning routine, went to a different workplace, did different things at work, went to a different church, and so forth. They enjoyed different foods and wore different clothes.

They were motivated by different principles and had different goals. They had a different purpose for living and a different image of themselves.

Wow!

Please read the last few paragraphs again and think about it.

It's amazing how different we can be from who we have been. Every single thing about us can be different. The great power of the human mind is such that we can transform completely from one being into another.

For most of us, this journey has taken place with only a few maps to guide us. In most cases we have a single goal at a time. We start out with a single goal. To be graduated from high school. Then college. Get a job. Get a better job. Move up. Get married. Buy house. And so forth. One goal at a time.

If you lay out a map on the table you can plot where you are and where you have been. And for most of us, we plot out one more dot for where we want to go next. Take a vacation. Refinance the house. Get ready for Christmas.

You could approach the future at a deeper level and plot a future point for each of three areas in your life:

Personal

Family

Work

Wait: It gets better. The most amazing thing about our human capacity is this: You can plot out a completely new you. A new job, a new house, a new life with new hobbies. New friends, new church, new exercise habits, new sex life, new books, new music. New whatever-you-want.

STOP. THINK.

This is very powerful. After all, when you look back at all the people you've been, you have to know that you will be a completely different person ten years from now. You'll have all those "new" things whether you plan it or not. The future's coming and there's nothing you can do to stop it. The new you is coming too, and you can do something about it.

Because most of us plot out one point at a time, we are bound by where we are now. We see the world from "here" and "now" instead of seeing that anything is possible. We limit our future vision because of our present circumstances. We don't have to behave this way.

If you read through this superficially, you may consider it interesting. Think about it in more detail and you will see that this is an earth-shaking proposition. It is life-creating. It is true and it has massive ramifications. Think about this perspective until you believe it. It will change your life.

You have the power to become anyone you want. If you are willing to lay out the plan, plot the course, and work at it, you can become the person you want to be.

This is a completely radical viewpoint for most of us. In fact, it's overwhelming. Where do you begin? You begin with the first major change in your life: Daily Reflection.

Let's assume you want to make this change. When you begin, you have no end-point. After all, when you begin the process of becoming anything you want, you should consider carefully before you decide. So you have to ask yourself some questions:

What am I doing?

    – What's the project?

Why am I doing this?

    – What are the benefits?

How did this get started?

    – What's my story? How did I get here?

I refer to the next you – the You that you want to become – as You2. To get started on the road to You2, you need two things. First, you need an end point, a " You2." You have to come up with a person you want to be. This will start out extremely vague and evolve over time, but you have to start somewhere.

Second, you need to start working on the details. There's a lot of work ahead. While you're defining who you want to become, you will need to develop a personal philosophy and some goals and habits. You will need to do a lot of thinking and some praying. There are a million changes ahead. You get to make all the decisions. You'll need rest. You'll need exercise. You'll need time to think and work on this.

You have to dedicate some time every day to work on your new life.

Here's how you used to map your life:

Now you're going to change your perspective completely:

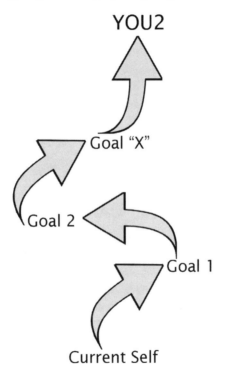

You have to create that You2 end point in your mind. This will take a lot of work.

At the same time you have to define where you are today. You need to evaluate everything about your current life. Some of it is wonderful and you'll want to keep that. Some things you'll want to change. Many many things you've never thought about. Many habits just evolved on their own. They need to be evaluated.

Do not be overwhelmed. We're going to take this one step at a time. Some things will be difficult. Change is never easy. But this change should not be scary. You're going to grab control of your life for the first time ever. You will be in complete control. You get to make all the decisions.

Take a deep breath. Don't overwhelm yourself right away. You can do this.

I have a friend who used to work for me. I hired him in 1993 when he was fresh out of college. He wanted to learn about technology (This was before the "World Wide Web" was popularized by Netscape). In those early days you had to teach yourself about the Internet. There weren't many books and even fewer good ones.

So I taught myself how to create Internet sites. And Stan would ask me to teach him. He saw the future and wanted to be part of it. So he asked, "Teach me, boss. Give me the power." I would show him some things and tell him how to teach himself, the way I had done it. I kept teaching myself, staying up on the new developments.

I designed systems and built Internet sites. He said "Teach me." Time passed. I moved on to other things. When the graphical World Wide Web was evolving in 1994, I built award-winning web sites. When I left that company, he took over a major function I had had. He did well but never taught himself the higher level skills.

I went on to do consulting. At one point I worked with a client who needed someone with a specific set of skills. I recommended Stan and he got the job. He learned the job quickly but continued to turn to me and say "Teach me." Five years after I met him, Stan was still asking me to teach him, as if I could open his head and reveal one or two secrets that keep my technical skills on the cutting edge.

In the meantime, I had spent a fortune on those big, 400-page computer books that cost $60 each. I'd read and read and read. I'd tried to get my hands on the "real world" software and teach myself how to do the things that needed to be done. I'd put in long days, long weeks, and long years teaching myself what I needed to know. For five years I'd worked my tail off to maintain a "cutting edge" level of knowledge.

And after five years Stan had never taken his technical knowledge to a higher level. Instead of digging in and teaching himself, he'd asked me. As if a few bits of information from me would make clear the knowledge he sought in every area of technology. He did well in his job, but he never taught himself what he needed to reach the next level.

Now it's more than ten years, and Stan just never moved very far in technology.

When you look back and say "It's been ten years," you have to believe that he could have found some time in that 120 months to train himself.

Time slips away. We can let it pass or we can work to reach our goals.

It is easy to put things off. It is easy every day to *not* work toward our goals. It is easy every day to *not* start the journey to our new selves. It is easy to let five years drift by.

When you look back ten years, you'll see that you are different from the person you used to be. Did you drift through the last ten years? Or did you plot a course and move in the direction you wanted to go?

Now, get started on the next five years and the next ten years.

You Are Who You Say You Are

One of the first things I learned as a consultant is that You Are Who You Say You Are. I went to a printer and got myself some business cards, stationary, and envelopes. With a few hundred dollars invested I could now look like an established business.

I've seen others do the same. I meet people from time to time who are just starting out but portray a sense of professionalism and experience beyond their actual time in the business. With a good perception and a positive attitude, they hope to get one good job. If they do well and make the customer happy, they can push for referrals and more jobs. And thus they become who they say they are.

In a similar way, we need to get up in the morning and "put on the uniform" for who we are today. I work about half time from my home office. When I started, I had to get in the habit of getting dressed for work every day, even if I knew I would be at home all day. I put on work clothes and I checked into my office by 8:30 AM every day. It's easier to "be" a business when I act like a business.

Alright, you say to yourself, what's this got to do with me? How can this approach help me?

We are always evolving. As people, as professionals, as technicians. At the same time, our habits hold us back. While our desires help us look to the next great challenge, our habits keep us comfortable in the present.

I've managed hundreds of people over the years and met all kinds of workers. Some are happy where they are and their driving force is to keep up with the work and be good at what they do. Others talk about advancement and somehow never do anything about it. Still others take night classes and ask for more responsibility and volunteer for work outside their current job description.

This last group is practicing being who they want to be. They take on the role of who they want to become.

In the fall of 2000 I decided to take my business to a higher level. I committed to hiring someone who had a fairly high level of technical certification. I put out an ad stating that Microsoft Certification is required. And the results were inspiring!

I divided the resumes into three groups. The first was people with no Microsoft Certification. These people were not eligible for the job. But they were being who they wanted to be. The second group consisted of people who were Microsoft Certified. Their experience varied widely.

The third group I had not anticipated. It consisted of people who had much more than a single certification. People in this group had passed a lot of exams and achieved the status of MCSE (Microsoft Certified Systems Engineers – The highest certification an individual can attain from Microsoft).

For the most part these people were "paper MCSEs." In other words, they took classes and passed exams, but they had little experience. This group was inspiring because their stories were all variations on a single theme: They had decided to change careers; they had set their goals on passing the Microsoft exams; and they had passed enough exams to reach the "big goal" of MCSE.

I interviewed several of these MCSEs and found that some of them had tried to move up in their organizations and couldn't. They had set their sites on a very difficult goal, put themselves through school at night, and achieved the goal. But now their bosses did not acknowledge this and let them advance in the technical area of their companies.

These people had transformed themselves into technical professionals. They became what they said they would. How sad that so many bosses failed to see and reward the kind of motivation and hard work we all say we want to encourage.

And at the same time this was very inspiring for me. This stack of resumes was not three or four or five. I had more than twenty-five resumes from these highly-motivated people. They had all put out a great deal of effort to transform themselves and had succeeded in becoming someone new. I wish I had the money to hire them all. What a great workforce that would be!

At the same time, I don't want to minimize the work involved. All of these people worked very hard to achieve the status of MCSE. We all have to work hard to become who we want to be.

Summary and Conclusions

Change happens to all of us all the time. Sometimes it is dramatic, but usually not. You will be different in a year and more different in two years.

If you focus your energy and work to become who you want to be, then you will use change to your advantage. If you do nothing, you can drift through the next year and let change happen without a guiding purpose. But you'll still change. If you take the second route, you don't know what change will do to you in the next year or two. But you can guess that you'll be a little fatter, a little lazier, and you will have caught up on those Andy Griffith reruns.

Change is going to happen. Help it, guide it, embrace it. Move always toward your goal and you'll get there. Your enemies are laziness, inertia, and lack of focus. Figure out where you want to go and get started today.

Here's step one:

Take a big felt marker and write "I want to change" on a piece of paper. Tape that on the wall where you'll see it every day. Now think about what kind of change you want. Write on a piece

> You are who you
> say you are: Who
> do you say you are?

of paper "What I want to Change:" and start making a list.

Perhaps you want to spend more time with your spouse or children. Maybe you want a 20% raise. Or Microsoft Certification. Whatever comes to mind, put it on the list. You might want a hundred things.

You can begin the process of consolidation and focusing your goals as soon as you have a few items on your list. But you have to have a list. You have to have a goal. Otherwise, you just get pushed this way and that way as change moves you along.

To Ponder

"The best investment is in the tools of one's own trade."
                                    – Benjamin Franklin

"Think of yourself as on the threshold of unparalleled success. A whole clear, glorious life lies before you. Achieve. Achieve."
                                    – Andrew Carnegie

"You don't have to control everything in order to change your destiny: You only have to change one or two little things about yourself."
                                    – Karl W. Palachuk

Chapter 11

The Muscles of Success

Introduction:
Muscle Memory

For ten years I played a consistently mediocre game of racquetball. I got to a certain level and, no matter how much
I played, I didn't get any better. Then one day I took a free
clinic at our racquet club and learned the proper way to hold
the racquet! My game improved instantly. I could serve
more accurately and with a great deal more power. I finally
understood how the really powerful players made it sound
like a gun going off when they served.

The basic problem was that I had taught myself "a" way to
hold the racquet, but I had not learned "the right way" to
hold the racquet.

I used to play with a guy who was raised in South Africa
and went to school in England. He had played racquetball
his entire life. I don't know why he played with me except
out of pity. He always knew where the ball was going. He
could instinctively judge the position and speed of the ball,

along with my movements, so he knew just where I'd hit the ball. He would walk over there and wait for it. Believe me, I got a lot more exercise than he did!

Let me clarify the use of the word "instinctively." My friend had learned from thirty years of playing racquetball. He had a vision of the game that I never developed. And he had "muscle memory" so that he didn't have to consciously decide which backhand shot to use or make a decision of how soft to hit the ball so it barely touched the front wall and then died.

In all athletic activity, we practice building muscle memory so that we can advance to the next level. Tennis players, golfers, weight lifters, and ballerinas all practice over and over so that they don't have to think about every muscle move when the time comes.

As the father of a gymnast I watched for years as my daughter did cartwheels along a straight piece of tape on the floor. And when it came time to do a cartwheel on a beam, she could! Of course, on a real beam there are additional skills to learn. The basic process of doing a cartwheel flawlessly on a straight line was now part of her unconscious activity – it was muscle memory. Now she could work on the next challenge.

Working on success, relaxation, and focus, also require this level of practice. You need to develop a sort of "Muscle Memory for Success." This has two parts.

First, you need to tune into the skills you learned *wrong* so you can re-learn them the *right way*.

Second, you need to practice the skills of success at your current level so you can move to the next level.

Unlearning What You Learned Wrong

When I learned racquetball, I held the racquet wrong at the beginning because I wanted to play the game. But holding the racquet incorrectly became a habit and soon enough it felt right to me. I couldn't move up to the next level until I moved back and relearned this skill.

Some people need to relearn communication skills or unlearn the habit of watching TV all night. Some need to unlearn wasteful spending habits and others need to unlearn the over-eating habit.

Take a moment and write down three or four things that you need to un-learn or re-learn the right way. Be patient with yourself. Remember, the muscle memory of success takes time. You may have developed a habit a long time ago and practiced it for ten years. You won't be able to re-learn that overnight. It is comfortable, even if you know it's wrong. To begin the process of re-learning, you will need to set some goals and begin practicing your new habits.

This is precisely the kind of activity that makes daily reflection useful. If you take ten minutes every day to review your goals for the day, you'll bring attention to your new undertaking. Focusing on your goals will bring them into your conscious mind and make your practice easier each day.

Develop New Skills of Success

Once you've established some goals and are focused forward on your own success, then you need to develop new skills of success: Taking time to relax; working hard when no one's looking; reading (reading, reading, reading); improving you job skills; goal-setting on a regular basis; exercising; and so forth.

Most of us instinctively know what we need to do to be successful, but it's easier to sleep in as late as possible, come home from work and plop down in front of the TV, sit like vegetables all night, and then do it all again the next day.

It takes discipline – and practice – to get up a little early, exercise, spend quiet time focusing on your goals for the day, reading in the evening, and consciously working on your success.

You also have to get to know the skills of success. You need to focus on the actions you take and acknowledge when you have a success. When you experience a success of any size, stop and savor it. Consider how it feels. How did you get here? How would you do it again? It feels good, doesn't it?

You need to focus on the feelings and actions of your success – these are your muscles of success. In order to exercise these muscles you have to be familiar with them.

You also must learn to use these "muscles" before you need them. Just like knowing the fire exits before the alarm goes off: You need to know how to use your muscles of success when the time comes.

Perhaps the hardest thing for most people to learn is relaxation. Most people have never spent time being wakeful and restful at the same time. There is great value in calming you mind and focusing on the moment. The more stressful the situation, the more important you will find this practice. But you can't practice when there's a stressful situation (like an irate customer yelling on the phone). You need to practice your calming technique before you need it. Then when you need it, it will be there for you. Your muscles will know what you want them to do.

Start today: Make a list of things you need to un-learn or re-learn. Make a list of successful practices you will work on. Then set aside the time and begin building muscle memory in the muscles of success.

Muscle Groups of Success

Now let's extend the analogy to the "Muscle Memory" of success.

You have Muscles of Success just as you have physical muscles. You need to exercise these muscles in order to have them "in shape." You need to build muscle memory so that you instinctively react in a successful way to any situation that pops up.

As you go through your day, you have a hundred routines that involve muscle memory. The way you grab your keys, lock the door, drive out of the driveway. You're on "autopilot." That's your muscles taking care of the routine so you don't have to focus your attention on all the details. You may have noticed how odd it seems when you move a piece of furniture, or get a new one. Suddenly, your automatic routine isn't automatic any more.

Sports rely heavily on muscle memory, particularly those involving equipment. Any activity in which "technique" matters is an activity in which muscle memory matters.

You practice your stance, your grip, your stroke, your focus – even your attitude.

In weight training, athletes work muscle groups. You may have heard the terms upper body and lower body. Even a relatively small area can have many muscles, so someone might work the upper arms, lower arms, muscles in the front, back, or side of the arms. If you can find a muscle in a physiology text, someone has a developed an exercise to build that muscle!

You need to have the same regimen with the muscles of success. There are two reasons to exercise the muscles of success. First, you need to build muscle memory. With muscle memory, the talents you need will be there when you need them.

The second reason to build your muscles of success is to develop the talents, skills, habits, and attitudes which you do not currently possess. Anyone who takes time to seriously consider the question will be able to list one or two areas that would increase their success. These might be sales skills, relationship skills, honesty skills, or many others.

Most people go into a line of work that interests them. It is natural that they have some talents and skills around their chosen field. But over time they realize that they need additional talents and skills. At critical points they get "stuck" where they are because they need to develop in some area.

This is most obvious for professionals – those who went to school for law, medicine, dentistry, or other specific jobs. In order to be successful, they have to learn how to run a business, manage people, deal with all the details of operating the business side of business. In other words, they now need to learn those important skills they didn't learn in professional school. The same thing happens to the rest of us too. We prepare for certain aspects of our career, then realize we need additional skills in order to reach the next level of success.

Often, we get stuck because we get comfortable and complacent. We want to stay right where we are. We don't want to develop new skills. We don't want to stretch or grow.

But despite the natural human love of inertia, the natural next step after a period of growth is that we become bored and restless. We feel stuck and want to make a change. Two things have happened. First, we developed a muscle of avoiding growth. This muscle can grow very strong in some people. Second, we have let several muscles atrophy – the muscles of inquisitiveness, learning, goal-setting, self-improvement, etc.

Just as with an athletic practice, we can all improve from where we are. A beginner, such as a new business owner who has to learn about managing people, can make quick progress. At the same time, an expert in some field can always continue learning and fine-tune the talents and habits that bring success.

When looking at the muscles of success that you need to develop, it is often useful to combine them into groups of related skills (or talents, habits, and attitudes). When we work on a group of related skills, we can make faster progress in all of them.

There are many ways to combine muscles of success into muscle groups of success. Perhaps the easiest is to look at one skill set and consider how you can improve in your personal life, family life, community life, and professional life. For example, if you wish to improve communication or punctuality, how can you improve this group across various aspects of your life?

One of my strongest convictions is that we should work to create a single self and not have a

> Me as parent
>
> Me as friend
>
> Me as professional
>
> Me at church
>
> Me at home
>
> Me as spouse
>
> etc.

As you work to combine a set of skills across the various aspects of your life, you work to synthesize your "selves" into a single YOU.

Another way to think about muscle groups is the combination of talents you need for a specific project or development phase. For example, in business there are skills related to finances and organizational structure. When I incorporated one of my businesses, I learned a lot about several skill areas in a short period of time.

A similar process happens when someone takes a new job or when two people get married. Suddenly, a large collection of related skills are needed. Obviously, the muscle group for a successful marriage involves a very different set of skills from the muscle group needed to be successful on the job.

Very often, muscle groups of success are already defined for us. Job descriptions or job objectives are simply a list of skills and talents needed for success on the job. But these descriptions are merely the bare minimum needed to do the job at a basic level. If you want to do a job excellently, you need to figure out the muscle groups of related habits and attitudes that will take your job to a higher plain.

> You need to work the muscles of success
> – including the dreaming muscle.

Of course you can get started today. Consider, what are the groups of skills, talents, habits, and attitudes that will bring you success? As with other elements of success, the process of considering these things will naturally bring you success.

Inventory the Muscles of Success

One day I was contemplating whether there's ever really a "short list" of habits or skills that one needs to be successful. So I started listing some Good Habits or personal traits that I've seen in the most successful people.

Please note for the record that success does not equal money. Most people can make more money in a short period of time if they are willing to give up some of the other elements of success: good relationships, a balanced life, etc. Success means attaining your goals. Okay, fine. The hard part is to actually do the work to decide what your goals are! You need to balance your goals as an individual, a professional, and a family member.

Of course that means life is complicated and the short list of habits or skills you need now has to be three or more short lists. What attributes do you need to be successful as a spouse or parent? On your job? In your personal life?

Remember, balancing your life will bring greater happiness and relaxation – and reduce stress! You don't have to outspend the budget. You don't have to work so hard that you're too exhausted to enjoy your family.

So the short list is a little longer. Here are the Muscles of Success I came up with in one session. I'm sure there are some I missed. Just like going to the gym to work your deltoids or abs, you can put your attention on one or two of these and "work" the Muscles of Success.

We all need to work on some or all of these Muscles of Success. Circle some attributes you know you need to work on. Circle as many as you need to work on. Make notes.

- Avoid Procrastination
- Be Decisive
- Be Efficient
- Be Energetic
- Be Great at Your Job
- Be Kind
- Be Temperate / Moderate
- Budget Time
- Compassion
- Control Your Ego
- Exercise
- Focus
- Exercise Your Imagination
- Follow-Up

- Find opportunities to teach and mentor rather than scold

- Have a Positive Attitude

- Meditate

- Passion

- Pay Your Dues

- Practice Fairness

- Practice Gratitude / Be Grateful

- Practice Selflessness

- Pray

- Reflect on Yesterday's Challenges

- Review your Finances

- Set Goals (long term, Monthly, Daily)

- Take Risks

- Work Hard

- Forgive

- Love

- Motivation

- Patience

- Persevere

- Plan each day (week, month, year)

- Practice Loyalty

- Practice Mindfulness – Focus on the moment

- Read

- Relax

- Render Services Fairly (give more than you're paid for)

- Take Pride in Your Work

- Tend to Relationships at Work

- Write Down Your Thoughts

If I missed any important habits, please email your suggestions to me at karlp@relaxfocussucceed.com.

I am firmly convinced that, with just a little thought, we all know what we need to do and what we need to change to be successful. The only thing we lack is motivation to make a plan and start working on it.

> ## God Loves Well-Rounded People

Many of us work very hard on the one thing that most defines our success. In other words, we become more successful in the one area that's easiest for us to be successful. But we are un-motivated in the areas where we find success more difficult. This might be the development of personal relationships or habits of kindness.

In other words, our tendency to focus where we've already found success leads us to an unbalanced life. We need goals in many areas. And one goal needs to be seeking the proper balance of the other goals.

> ## No One Can Motivate You! – You Have to Motivate Yourself!

Learning to Make Your Own Cookies

Who's Responsible For Your Happiness?

Let's take a moment to look at the topic of making ourselves happy and keeping ourselves happy. Please note for the record that we can't be happy all the time. It's not the natural order of things.

Stuff happens. Sometimes stuff happens to you. Being happy all the time is unreasonable. But dealing with life's little challenges should be manageable for everyone. You can't control every situation, but you have complete control over how you react.

There are only two reasons why you wouldn't have control over how you react. One is that you've decided not to have control. You let yourself be controlled by your environment. If the world pushes you, you push back.

> **We need to feel comfortable slowing down and taking in life.**

Second, you haven't thought about how you want to react, or the type of person you want to be, and therefore you have no choice but to respond to events as they occur.

Central to the Relax Focus Succeed® approach to life is taking time to learn about yourself. Far too many people – even otherwise successful people – don't know much about themselves. They don't know who they are, what they want, what's important in their lives, or why they do the things they do. They spend all of their lives reacting to the world around them.

Always reacting means never being in control. It means never taking control. It means letting anything and anybody decide what your life is like. Feeling helpless and out of control can lead to lot of negative behavior. Taking control of yourself and how you respond to the world around you is 100% within your control. It's a great place to start turning things around because it's guaranteed to be successful. You have the power to make this choice.

Of course you have a lifetime of habits and behavior that need to be replaced with new, positive, successful habits. And today's a great day to start!

I remember an old Peanuts cartoon in the newspaper. One of the kids asks "What do you do when you feel that life is treating you unfairly?" Snoopy responds "Learn to bake your own cookies."

There's a lot of truth in that.

Baking cookies can be categorized as part engaging activity, part comfort food, and part distraction from the troubles of life. We all need engaging and distracting activities to keep our lives balanced. If we get food out of the deal, that's just a bonus.

When we take the time to stop and consider it, life is a continuing series of actions and reactions, constantly intertwining and affecting each other. When we don't stop to think about it – when we let the events of life begin to overwhelm us – we begin to view things as "me against the world."

When we start down that path, we begin to see life as a series of events that happen to us rather than a set of things we can influence and control.

When the world comes crushing down (when life treats you unfairly), the solution is a little perspective. Taking time to bake cookies might be just what you need. Or gardening, or reading, or any other "puttering" activity.

When you pick an activity, remember that it must be engaging and distracting. It should be something that keeps you from focusing on the problems and worries of life. Doing one kind of work to keep yourself from focusing on another kind of work is not the answer. You need to do *non-work* in order to keep yourself from focusing on any work.

It's fine if your work is also your hobby. You're lucky if that's the case. But you still need something else to do to when the worries of work start to grow too large.

Exercise is a great distraction. Running, bicycling, lifting weights, aerobics, swimming, or whatever you enjoy. In addition to helping you get some perspective on life, it will help you live longer! Even non-aerobic exercise is proving to be extremely beneficial for your health. You don't have to be a world-class athlete to get benefits from exercise. You just have to do something.

Comfort Food

And let's not forget the final element of baking cookies (or whatever distraction you choose): comforting yourself. If you hang around new parents you may hear them discussing whether a child has discovered a way to "comfort himself." Very often this means thumb-sucking or some other very simple activity.

When a baby learns to comfort himself, then he can calm himself and go back to sleep after being startled or waking up and realizing that he's alone. This is a wonderful skill.

Unfortunately, many of us seem to have lost the skill of comforting ourselves as we get older. Sometimes we just never try. We ignore or avoid uncomfortable situations.

At other times we simply react to the situation at hand without thinking about it. We're frustrated, so we respond with frustration. We think the service is bad and we respond with anger. Traffic is tied up and we respond with rage.

> Unfortunately, many of us seem to have lost the skill of comforting ourselves . . .

The traits of self control and "think before you speak" seem to have been lost by modern society. We're always going and never stopping. We need to give ourselves that minute to think. We need to feel comfortable slowing down and taking in life.

We need to slow down just enough to process things and decide how to react. That way we participate in life rather than merely react to it. Slowing down and processing events are habits that need to be cultivated.

Start today. Take a few minutes to spend quiet time thinking about how you react to the world – especially when you feel a great deal of pressure. Do you react the way you'd like to? If not, why not?

> "A man who truly wants to make the world better should start by improving himself and his attitudes."
> – Fred DeArmond

Work slowly. Don't worry. You don't need to be perfect (soon or ever). But the process of working on yourself automatically makes you happier and more in control. It's like making your own cookies.

The Evolution of Understanding

This is certainly one of my favorite topics.

As I mentioned earlier, I'm a real believer in behavior.

For example, it doesn't matter why people stop at the stop signs. They might be afraid of getting a ticket, or being a bad example for their children, or just afraid of getting in an accident. It doesn't matter. The only thing that matters is *that* they stop at the stop sign.

Success is the same way. It doesn't matter why you have bad habits, or haven't developed the muscles of success. What matters is that you start today to develop these muscles.

I have a technician in my consulting practice who is easily "hijacked." He will go into a client to do one task (e.g., install software) and they will jump all over him when he comes in the door. "Oh, we're sooooo glad you're here. We need this printer moved. And the scanner's not delivering files to my desktop. We're going to be changing email providers this afternoon. My monitor's a little too green. . . ."

The overwhelming tendency in my business is to jump in and do all this work. And that's why so many people don't make a profit. With properly trained muscles of success, the tech needs to *not* jump in and do the work. First, we make a list of tasks. They get entered into our workflow system. Second, each is assigned a priority. Third, we estimate the time we'll be at the client. And Fourth, the tech needs to contact the service manager because it's the service manager who schedules time.

This is really very simple, and can be done quickly. But it has to be done. If the tech was scheduled to be onsite for half an hour, and it's now going to be three hours, the rest of the day needs to be rescheduled.

The key to success in this situation is that the technician needs to develop an "automatic" reaction to take control of the situation, organize it, and coordinate with the rest of the service team. He needs to develop those muscles of success so that "muscle memory" takes over. His old habit of simply reacting and doing may leave the rest of the service team in a reactive mode for the rest of the day.

There are levels of understanding and living the rules that lead us to success. First, you hear the rules and try to remember enough of them to do your job. Then, you find that you remember the rules and try very hard to do all of them. At some point, you have experiences that make you clearly understand why we have these rules. You may even have a very bad experience because you didn't follow the rules.

So you see, it doesn't matter why you follow the rules. At first you follow them because someone said so. Over time your understanding and commitment grows. Eventually, you preach the rules to others so that they will have success. It is possible that everyone is following the rules for a different reason, with a different level of understanding, and with a different level of commitment.

But if everyone does the things that make the organization successful, then the organization will be successful.

A similar thing happens in your personal life. The most famous person to tell you to go to bed, get a good night's sleep, and wake up early was Benjamin Franklin. But you'll find a hundred successful people echoing this same message – including your mother.

So that's one of the nearly-universal rules of success. You've heard it. You know it. Now you need to do it, even if you don't believe it will make you more successful. Begin doing it. Make it a habit. Build that muscle of success. At some point you will look back at the positive impact this behavior has had on your life. At that point you will begin teaching it to others.

It doesn't matter whether you practice successful behavior because you hope it will help, you believe it will help, or you know it will help. Practicing successful behavior will make you successful.

Summary and Conclusions

You've probably guessed by now that this entire chapter is really just about habits. You've heard it said a hundred different ways: successful habits make successful people.

In the big overview, it is easy to see your bad habits. For example, if you watch television six hours a day, you'll be really good at watching TV. When you decide that you want to stop talking about improving your life, and begin working on improving your life, that habit will need to change.

Determining the list of good habits is another story. While there are some universal habits of success, you also need to find the few key habits that will be the focal point of *your* success. And that requires one other element: a well-defined set of values, principles, and goals.

Now we've come full circle with the goal-setting and value-setting discussion. If you say you value education and training, how does that manifest itself in your *actions*.

What verbs get the biggest workout in your daily diary? You know, action words. Behavior. Actions. Activities.

Is there consistency between your values and your actions? If you said you value your family, how much attention do they get? If you value giving time to the community, how much do you give?

The really great news about taking time to think about all these activities is that they build on one another. Every time you take time look at the big picture (actions, values, principles), you build a higher level of consistency to your life. That reduces stress, makes you more successful, and prepares you to move to the next level.

As you "master" certain habits, you will have moved your muscle exercises from the conscious to the unconscious realm. When you've built up the muscles of success so that you have complete muscle memory in one area, then you're ready to work on the next set of muscles. Now your exercise will consist of an occasional tune-up on the things you do well and concentrated effort on your next level of success.

Very early on I wrote that success is like a religion. You don't check it off your list and mark it as "done." No, you have to work on it every day. Sometimes you'll slide backward. Don't worry about it. Pick yourself up, be kind and forgiving to yourself, and go back to it the next day.

You really get to start over every day with a clean slate. The hardest part is getting started.

To Ponder

"The only conquests that are permanent and leave no regrets are our conquests over ourselves."
                    – Napoleon Bonaparte

"Reflect on your life. The greatest joys and sorrows of your life are a direct result of change. The greatest victories and defeats are a result of change. And yet most of us don't have a philosophy toward change."
                    – Karl W. Palachuk

"The victory of success is half won when one gains the habit of work."
                    – Sarah Bolton

Chapter 12

Daily Exercises and Journaling

Introduction

This chapter provides a few activities you can do to help you along your way. These are ideas for Quiet Time activities.

When you start out with a commitment to spend 30-60 minutes a day in quiet time, there are many ways you can use that time. But sometimes you'll get bored, or tired of the same old thing. Here are some ideas to fill your year with activities and make your quiet time useful.

Types of Quiet Time

I used to try to create a schedule for my quiet time. Now I sit down, settle in, and decide what I'm in a mood for. Here are the most common things I end up doing:

Read (Non-work stuff. Self improvement is good.)

Write

Review goals

Meditate

    Relax

    Pain

    Mindfulness

Guided

Pray

Physical exercise (e.g., walking <u>without</u> a CD player or MP3 player).

Quiet Time should always start with a settling-in routine. Sit down, get comfortable. Close your eyes and take a few deep breaths. Calm yourself and make sure you're in the mood to work on "you."

I recommend that you do a variety of things. Don't focus on goals to the exclusion of other things; don't exercise to the exclusion of other things, etc.

Here are a few tips on what you should *not* do. Do not work on work. Don't take spreadsheets or drafts of letters to read. This is not just a quiet time to get work done (If you need that, schedule it separately).

Don't work on "issues" or problems. If you wish to introduce these things and let your mind wander, that's fine. But don't sit down specifically to solve a problem. Sit down and let your mind do what it wants to do.

Meditations

In addition to getting CDs, tapes, and MP3s to guide you through meditations, you can certainly come up with your own. All this really means is that you follow this simple process and focus on the topic of your choice:

Sit down / settle in

Cleansing breaths

Read or think about the specific meditation. Formulate what you want to think about.

Close your eyes and consider the topic from as many perspectives as possible.

(If you need a timer to keep track of time, get a kitchen timer that's not too obnoxious.)

When the meditation time is up, gradually come back to full consciousness.

Don't expect to "find" answers when you meditate on something. You will, eventually, find answers. But don't expect them to show up in any thirty minute session.

Exercise One: What makes you happy today?

Inspired by the discussion in Chapter One.

Read the following passage. Then close your eyes and think about it for some time. If you have any inspiring thoughts you don't want to forget, take a minute and write them down.

When I ask you what makes you happy today, there are two possible answers. The first answer is superficial – it's the parlor game level of self-awareness. You might say money, or sex, or time to go on a date with your spouse. I'm not saying that this superficial answer is untrue, but it is probably trite. It doesn't have any personal meaning for you and the answer could be different tomorrow and the day after that.

The other answer you can give is a well-considered, principle-centered reflection of who you are and what you value. This statement does not have to be long and complicated. It need not involve a lengthy discussion of the relative importance of competing values in your life. In fact, the "true" answer to what makes you happy can be short and sweet. For example, "My family makes me happy."

Tip: To get the most out of an exercise like this, it is best to repeat it several days in a row. You might do as few as three or four, or as many as thirty.

Exercise Two: You Are Who You Say You Are

Inspired by the discussion in Chapter Ten

One of the easiest ways to make a change is to begin describing yourself in the new way. People who start their own businesses learn this really fast. One day you wake up and say "I am . . . <your new career>." This simple tool helps you to see the new you.

Read through this exercise. Then close your eyes and think about the following questions for 10-15 minutes. Write down your answers.

- Who are you?

- What are you?

- Who will you be?

- What do you want to be?

- Why aren't you there now?

Exercise Three: The Muscles of Success

Inspired by the discussion in Chapter Eleven.

Read through this exercise. Then close your eyes and think about the following questions for 10-15 minutes. Write down your answers.

We all need to work on some or all of these Muscles of Success. Circle some attributes you know you need to work on. Circle as many as you need to work on. Make notes.

- Avoid Procrastination
- Be Decisive
- Be Efficient
- Be Energetic
- Be Great at Your Job
- Be Kind
- Be Temperate/Moderate
- Budget Time
- Compassion
- Control Your Ego
- Exercise
- Exercise Your Imagination

- Find opportunities to teach and mentor rather than scold

- Focus

- Follow-Up

- Forgive

- Have a Positive Attitude

- Love

- Meditate

- Motivation

- Passion

- Patience

- Pay Your Dues

- Persevere

- Plan each day (week, month, year)

- Practice Fairness

- Practice Gratitude/ Be Grateful

- Practice Loyalty

- Practice Mindfulness – Focus on the moment

- Practice Selflessness

- Pray

- Read

- Reflect on Yesterday's Challenges

- Relax

- Render Services Fairly (give more than you're paid for)

- Review your Finances

- Set Goals (long term, Work

- Take Pride in Your Monthly, Daily)

- Take Risks

- Tend to Relationships at Work

- Work Hard

- Write Down Your Thoughts

Exercise Four: Form Good Habits and Become Their Slave

Read this through when you wake up in the morning and then sit quietly and contemplate it's meaning for 10-15 minutes. Then, find some quiet time before you go to sleep at night and read through it again. Consider how these thoughts helped you focus your actions and your life.

> Og Mandino has said "Form good habits and become their slave." But be aware that you also become the slave of your bad habits. The good news is that you have the power to drop old habits and acquire new ones every day.
>
> This is easier said than done, however. We are slaves to our habits precisely because they become part of who we are. It's easy to say "Drop that bad habit." It's much more difficult to say "Change who I am."
>
> Think about one bad habit you want to drop and one good habit you want to acquire. Write them down on large piece of paper and post it on the wall so you see it every day.

Repeat as needed. I bet your habits begin to change. I've heard it said that it takes 42 days to pick up a new habit. Test that theory.

Exercise Five: Dream Elaborately

Read this through when you wake up in the morning and then sit quietly and contemplate it's meaning for 10-15 minutes. Then, find some quiet time before you go to sleep at night and read through it again. Consider how these thoughts helped you focus your actions and your life. Repeat for 30 days.

This month-long meditation should be fun. After all, who doesn't like to dream?

> Sit quietly and think about one or your dreams – a big dream. Begin to consider the details. What color, how much, who will help, how does that piece fit? Let yourself consider the details. Swim in the details.

> Even after one or two days, you will not be able to make it through your day without coming back to the dream. You will begin to see seemingly-unrelated experiences in a new light.

> You can change dreams every day or every few days. If you meditate on the same dream for a week, almost everything you do will somehow seem to be related to the dream.

> And another thing will happen: You'll start to take steps outside the dream world. You'll see whether that financing is really possible, and how much printing costs, and which resources are available. You'll gather real-world data that will make your dreams even more elaborate.

> You might actually begin to make your dream come true!

Exercise Six: Spin Doctor

Read this through when you wake up in the morning and then sit quietly and contemplate it's meaning for 10-15 minutes. Repeat for one week.

> Interpreting events in a positive light is a powerful skill. But for some it is also difficult. It took years of practice to interpret the world as you do. It will take much practice and discipline to interpret it differently.
>
> Begin each day with a commitment to be your own "spin doctor." Interpret the actions and interactions of your life in a positive light. Meditate each day on the usefulness of focusing on the moment and not on history.

Each night, take a few minutes to evaluate how you did. Consider how these thoughts helped you focus your actions and your life. This is an extremely difficult habit to change. Be kind to yourself. Take your time.

Exercise Seven: Inventory of Success

Read this through when you wake up in the morning and then sit quietly and contemplate it's meaning for 10-15 minutes. Repeat for one week.

> One of the most important elements of your success is your faith in yourself and your belief that your past accomplishments will serve you well as you move ahead.

Begin each day by making a list of a few things that support you on your journey: talents, recent successes, people who love you, skills, certifications, and so forth. Don't try to list everything all at once, just 3-5 per day.

For each element of your success, consider how it helped you get where you are and how it might be useful in the day ahead.

Each night, take a few minutes to evaluate how these 3-5 items helped you today. Be thankful.

Hint: Don't worry if you keep coming up with some repeats. While it's a good exercise to list all the hundreds of things that give us support every day, that's not what this exercise is about. In addition, most of us find that we have a few key talents (etc.) that help us to be successful every day.

Journaling

One of the handiest things you can do is to get yourself a blank pad of paper and take it with you during quiet time. You can buy blank journals at most book stores.

I prefer the little 6 x 9 mini-legal pads. They're not cumbersome, and it's handy to jot down each new idea on a new page. I think I'd be less inclined to do that with a large tablet.

I don't keep a daily diary-type journal. But I do try to write a bit every day about my thoughts, and I date the pages. If they turn out to be just random thoughts, I throw them in one drawer. If I think they'd be useful, I put them in another drawer.

What constitutes useful?

For me, an idea that might become an article is useful. Thoughts about my long-, medium- and short-term goals are useful. Sometimes I find myself writing notes to my wife. Those are usually useful.

I even keep some items in common folders. For example, anything related to goals, vision, values, and that sort of thing goes in one folder. Possible meditations go in another folder.

If you take on a longer meditation project (e.g., consider the same question for thirty days), then journaling your thoughts is very useful.

If you have a visible goal you work on over time, journaling about your progress is useful. For example, if you want to do 240 minutes of exercise per week, you might log your minutes and activities every day, along with any thoughts you have about the process.

Journaling is an important part of the Relax Focus Succeed® process because it's tied to introspection: Looking at yourself and thinking about yourself. One of the themes throughout this book has been self assessment. Remember: The unexamined life is not worth living!

This little habit – introspection – is what separates the top 1% from everyone else. Think about your life. Think about how *this* action fits with *that* goal. Think about how individual relationships fit in the big picture.

Think about everything. Just like any other muscle of success, the process of evaluating yourself in a useful way becomes easier over time. Journaling is key to this because writing down your thoughts requires you to organize them enough to understand what you wrote.

Writing down your thoughts helps you to articulate them. They become clearer to you and easier to describe to others. Sometimes you'll look at the written word and wonder "Wow. Do I really believe that?"

And most surprising of all, writing down your thoughts and plans and dreams makes it possible for you to look back years later. It allows you to see where you were, and where you thought you'd be today. So, I guess, it can keep you on track for your goals.

Exercise Eight: A Pain Journal

Inspired by my rheumatoid arthritis.

If you have significant pain of any kind, keeping a journal can be helpful. At one point in time, I was keeping a "Pain Journal." I wrote down every day where I felt pain. Hands, feet, hips, elbows. I also wrote the pain level on a scale of one to ten.

Why is this useful? Precisely because most of us don't think about pain enough. Pain is the unwelcome and unusual visitor in our lives. It arrives, we work through it, and it departs.

But sometimes pain is chronic (this is true for emotional pain as well as physical pain). When pain is chronic, you need to find a way to live with it.

Meditations on pain, and journaling, will help you define the pain. I'll use foot pain as an example.

> Where is the pain? Does it go down to the
> toes? All the toes? Is it in the ball of the foot?
> In the ankle?
>
> Its it steady, or does it come and go? Is it sharp
> or dull? Does it move around?
>
> Is there a way you can hold your foot that feels
> better? Does it feel better when you rub it? Does
> it feel better with your shoes on or off?
>
> And so forth.

As odd as it may sound to someone who hasn't gone through
it, defining your pain can reduce the level of pain and make
it much easier to live with.

I always advise consultants: The worst pain is the pain you
don't expect. Of course, that advice is related to consulting.
If you warn a client that they have a big expense coming
down the road, it will hurt less when the time comes.

The same is true of physical pain (and emotional pain).
Know it and understand it. You may not be able to conquer
it, but you can keep it in perspective and know what its
boundaries are.

Summary and Conclusions

You obviously don't have to have my routine. You don't
have to do the things I do.

But I encourage you to do something. Take some time to
read, to write, to meditate, to pray, and to get some exercise.
Pick a combination that works for you.

Take time to be by yourself. Take a little retreat every day. Work on being the next person you want to be.

To Ponder

"A goal that is not written down is no better than a passing thought."
                    – Karl W. Palachuk

"Habit and routine have an unbeliev-able power to waste and destroy."
                    – Henri de Lubac

"Habit is a cable; we weave a thread of it each day, and at last we cannot break it."
                    – Horace Mann

Chapter 13

Final Thoughts

A Few Last Notes

Everyone deserves a happy, healthy, fulfilling life. And the truth is , such a life is within everyone's grasp.

The philosophy of Relax Focus Succeed® is very simple. We need to slow down in order to get more accomplished. We need to take time to focus our attention on what's important in our lives. We need to work on our own success.

Our modern society has us running around, often at full speed, scurrying to accomplish *something*. Almost no one takes the time to stop and consider where they want to go and what they want to be.

I'm frequently asked how relaxing is going to help accomplish anything. I hope you can see that it's the absolute key to success. It is only when we take some time to look inside ourselves and decide what's important that we can begin to achieve it.

To do that, we need to stop running around, turn off the television, and consciously work on our future. Whether we call it goal-setting or something else, we need the process of knowing where we're going.

And, fundamentally, what do we gain by this process? Focus!

If relaxation is the key to success, then focus is the first reward. Focus – the ability to concentrate your attention and your effort – is a true super power that you possess. You just need to know how to use it.

I say focus is the first reward because, once you begin the process of relaxing and figuring out what you want to be, the first thing that happens is focus. At that point, most people back off, get lazy, and don't follow through.

They check the box that says

And then they move on to doing something else. As time

> ☑ Set goals for my life.

goes on, the focus fades and life becomes pointless and meandering again. I hope this doesn't happen to you.

Success means reaching your goals. Focus is the super power that will get you there. The more you focus, the faster you'll accomplish your goals.

Accomplishing all of this starts out from a very simple activity. You may think it starts with a big, grand gesture. No, it starts with relaxing and going through the process of getting to know yourself.

The Wolf You Feed

The following story was passed on to me as a bit of Cherokee Wisdom. I don't know any more about its origins.

Two Wolves

> One evening an old Cherokee told his grandson about a battle that goes on inside people.
>
> He said, "My son, the battle is between two wolves inside us all.
>
> One is Evil. It is anger, envy, jealousy, sorrow, regret, greed, arrogance, self-pity, guilt, resentment, inferiority, lies, false pride, superiority, and ego.
>
> The other is Good. It is joy, peace, love, hope, serenity, humility, kindness, benevolence, empathy, generosity, truth, compassion and faith."
>
> The grandson thought about it for a minute and then asked his grandfather: "Which wolf wins?"
>
> The old Cherokee simply replied, "The one you feed."

As we begin rebuilding ourselves and preparing to move to the next stage in our lives, it is good to occasionally evaluate which wolf we're feeding.

Our tendency as humans is to experience "positive" emotions together and "negative" emotions together. So, when we feel frustrated, we're more susceptible to also feel angry and depressed. When we feel happy, we're more open to feeling grateful and loving.

Sometimes when you're in a funk – feeling the darker emotions – you need to just let it wear itself out. But you can also force yourself away from the negative emotions and toward the positive.

More and more research is showing that you can actually make yourself happier and give yourself a more positive mental attitude by doing the things that happier, more positive people do. Even if you're not a big jokester, exposing yourself to humor and things that make you laugh will help you to be more happy and less sad.

This is definitely not the kind of thing you want to solve with a pill. Pills that make you happy also tend to have all kinds of unwanted side effects. Intoxication leads to hangover.

It is much better to train yourself to trigger more happiness and less anger. Parents of very young children know that there are times when you simply cannot do anything to help a baby stop crying. At some point, the child has to learn to comfort herself.

Well we, as adults, need to do the same thing. But too often adults comfort themselves with alcohol or drugs. We don't really learn to comfort ourselves, we simply learn to medicate ourselves.

One of the great benefits of daily quiet time is that you learn the habit of quieting your mind and your body. You know what it feels like and you learn how to get into that state. So, when the world comes beating at your door and the "dark" wolves want to be fed, you know how to go, have some quiet time, and take control of your emotional health.

It is also important to evaluate who you spend time with. At work, in your personal life, at school. Everywhere.

Do you hang around with angry people who seem never to be happy? Or people who seem to ruin every personal relationship they have? If so, you'll get caught up in that negativity.

You can't fix other people. The best you can hope for is that they decide to make some changes and ask for help.

Perhaps one of the most difficult things a person can do it to change the people he spends time with. In our culture, it just doesn't feel "right" to cut people off, move away, and separate yourself from them.

Just remember, our culture is also not good at recognizing that you need to take care of yourself, reward yourself, and nurture yourself. If you don't take care of yourself first, you can't properly care for others. Sometimes that means you need to separate yourself from certain people.

Some people will simply waste your time. Some will lead you down the wrong path. Others will keep you motivated and feeling good.

Spend time with people who love you and nurture you and support you. Move away from those who whine and complain and feed the bad wolf.

There are many ways we can feed the good wolf. We can reward ourselves, try to laugh every day, build positive habits, and work to achieve them. If nothing else, it helps to realize that there are two sets of habits and that you get to choose which you will nurture.

I encourage you to spend some quiet time building two lists, the evil wolf and the good wolf. Write down as many behaviors as you can think of on each list. Then consider which of these represents where you are now, and which represents where you want to be.

Good luck. Be kind to yourself. It's hard work, but it's worthwhile.

Summary and Conclusions

I can't say that there's one road to success because I know there are many. I can't say I know *your* path to success. But I know that you can determine your path success.

We must each find our own path to happiness, fulfillment, and financial security. This is hard work. It's serious work. This is the most important work you have to do in your life. Once you do this work, all the other work is possible and meaningful.

This important work never stops. You have to do this work every day. Remember, you're fighting the natural human instinct to throw more horsepower – more labor – at your problems. You know that's counter-productive, but you want to do it.

The essential elements of your success are:

- Regular quiet time
  - To plan and set goals

- To evaluate where you are, where you've been, and where you're going

- To read and contemplate and "do nothing" so your brain has a chance to relax and do the important work

• Regular exercise

- So you can keep your human shell in working order

• Dedicated attention – focus – on your goals

- To keep your goals in mind

- To regulate your behavior

- To change your habits and keep your daily actions consistent with your stated goals

Our habits are our best friend and our worst enemy. They are completely within our control. And we are completely within their control.

At the same time, you will discover lots of "right" things that you need to do. These habits will help you achieve your goals. They are the muscles of your success and you need to spend time exercising them.

You, and only you, have the power to change your habits. In an instant, you can decide to change all of your habits. Of course it may take time to actually change those habits. You need to focus every day on being the person you want to be.

Relaxing, focusing, succeeding. This is very hard work.

It is also the path to the most rewarding experience you will ever have in your life. Think about it this way: You get to figure out what you want to do and what will make you the happiest, most fulfilled person on earth. Then you get to go do that.

You set the standards. You set the goals. You determine the path to take. And you determine what constitutes winning.

If you follow this simple system, you cannot lose.

You can only win.

Earlier I wrote that I have every excuse not to exercise. The same is true with quiet time. I have every excuse not to set goals; not to spend ten minutes deciding how my day will go.

> Do it.

> Do it every day.

> Just do it.

I sincerely hope that you will work through the exercises in this book. Try it for a month. You will be amazed at how much difference it makes in your life.

Try if for a year. Write down your goals and thoughts. Maybe keep a journal. After a year you'll be astounded at how different your life is.

I am sad that most people will never try these exercises. Perhaps only ten percent will try. With luck, five percent will stick with it for a month. Who will build the habits to work on their habits for a year?

As I write this, I've been working on regular "Relax Focus Succeed" activities for seven years. I believe every major accomplishment I have is a result of these activities.

Please try it. Please stick with it. Please contact me at www.Relax-FocusSucceed.com and let me know how things are going.

You have a lot of hard work ahead of you - and rewards beyond your wildest dreams.

Enjoy.

– Karl P.

To Ponder

"There is only one success: To be able to spend your life in your own way."
– Christopher Morley

"Waste of time is the most extravagant of all expense."
– Theophrastus

"Where you find consistency between your values and your actions, there you will find personal fulfillment and happiness."
– Karl W. Palachuk

Resources

Great Books

Recommended Books – The Relax Focus Succeed® Reading List

There are so many great books on improving yourself and fulfilling your life that I had a hard time putting together a short list. On the web site (www.relaxfocussucceed.com) you'll find dozens of other books.

But I want to give you good direction (good focus) and not dilute it with a long list of places to "start." So here's what I call the A List. These are all truly great books, and each is a great place to start.

The A List:

Jack Canfield, Leslie Hewitt, Mark Victor Hansen, *The Power of Focus*.

Stephen R. Covey, A. Roger Merrill, and Rebecca R. Merrill, *First Things First: To Live, to Love, to Learn, to Leave a Legacy.*

Wayne W. Dyer, *The Power of Intention: Learning to Co-Create Your World Your Way.*

Michael Gerber, *The E-Myth Revisited.*

Og Mandino, *The Greatest Secret in the World.*

Other Works Mentioned

The Bible

Chicken Soup for the Soul books (various authors).

Richard Carlson, *Don't Sweat the Small Stuff at Work.*

Wade Cook, *Don't Set Goals (The Old Way).*

Stephen Covey, *The 7 Habits of Highly Effective People.*

Dean Edell, *Eat, Drink, & Be Merry.*

Keith Ellis, *The Magic Lamp: Goal Setting for People Who Hate Setting Goals.*

Michael Gerber, *The E-Myth Contractor.*

Laurie Beth Jones, *The Path.*

John Main, *Moment of Christ.*

Thomas Merton, *No Man is An Island.*

Andrew Postman, *There's Always Time for Greatness: Who Did What When From Ages 1-100.*

Shinzen Young, Audio CD: *Break Through Pain.*

List of Values

This is certainly not a complete, or unique list of values. But it's a place to start.

Abundance	Charm	Directness	Frankness
Acceptance	Chastity	Discipline	Freedom
Accomplishment	Cheerfulness	Discretion	Friendliness
Accountability	Clarity	Dominance	Frugality
Accuracy	Cleanliness	Dreaming	Fun
Achievement	Clear-mindedness	Drive	Gallantry
Activeness	Cleverness	Duty	Generosity
Adaptability	Closeness	Dynamic	Gentility
Advancement	Collaboration	Eagerness	Giving
Adventure	Comfort	Education	Goodness
Affection	Commitment	Effectiveness	Gratitude
Affluence	Communication	Efficiency	Gregariousness
Aggressiveness	Community	Elegance	Growth
Agility	Compassion	Empathy	Happiness
Alertness	Competence	Encouragement	Harmony
Altruism	Competition	Endurance	Health
Ambition	Composure	Energetic	Helpfulness
Amusement	Confidence	Enjoyment	Heroism
Approachability	Conformity	Entertainment	Holiness
Assertiveness	Consistency	Enthusiasm	Honesty
Attentiveness	Contentment	Equality	Honor
Attractiveness	Continuity	Excellence	Hopefulness
Audacity	Control	Excitement	Hospitality
Authority	Cooperation	Exhilaration	Humility
Awareness	Coordination	Expediency	Humor
Balance	Courage	Expertise	Imagination
Beauty	Courtesy	Exploration	Impact
Belonging	Craftiness	Extravagance	Impartiality
Benevolence	Creativity	Extroversion	Improvememt
Bliss	Credibility	Exuberance	Independence
Boldness	Cunning	Fairness	Industry
Bravery	Curiosity	Faith	Influence
Brilliance	Decisiveness	Fame	Ingenuity
Calmness	Decorum	Family	Innovation
Camaraderie	Democracy	Fearlessness	Inquisitiveness
Candor	Dependability	Ferocity	Insightfulness
Capability	Determination	Fidelity	Inspiration
Carefulness	Devotion	Fierceness	Integrity
Certainty	Devoutness	Fitness	Intellectual
Challenging	Difference	Flexibility	Intelligence
Change	Dignity	Focus	Intensity
Charity	Diligence	Fortitude	Intimacy

Introversion
Intuitiveness
Inventiveness
Judiciousness
Justice
Kindness
Knowledge
Leadership
Learning
Liberty
Liveliness
Logic
Longevity
Love
Loyalty
Maturity
Mellowness
Merit
Meticulousness
Mindfulness
Modesty
Money
Mysteriousness
Non-violence
Obedience
Open-mindedness
Openness
Optimism
Order
Organization
Originality
Outlandishness
Outrageousness
Passion
Peace
Perceptiveness
Perfection
Perkiness
Perseverance
Persistence
Persuasiveness
Philanthropy
Piety
Playfulness
Pleasantness
Pleasure
Poise
Polish
Popularity

Power
Practicality
Pragmatism
Precision
Preparedness
Privacy
Professionalism
Progress
Prosperity
Prudence
Punctuality
Purity
Quality
Realism
Reason
Reasonableness
Recognition
Refinement
Reflection
Regularity
Relaxation
Reliability
Religion
Reputation
Resilience
Resourcefulness
Respect
Responsibility
Responsiveness
Rest
Restraint
Results-oriented
Reverence
Risk
Romance
Sacrifice
Safety
Saintliness
Satisfaction
Security
Self-control
Self-reliance
Self-respect
Selflessness
Sensitivity
Sensuality
Serenity
Service
Sexuality

Shrewdness
Silence
Simplicity
Sincerity
Skillfulness
Solitude
Sophistication
Speed
Spirituality
Spontaneity
Spunk
Stability
Standardization
Stillness
Strength
Success
Support
Supremacy
Surprise
Sympathy
Teamwork
Temperance
Thankfulness
Thoroughness
Thoughtfulness
Thrift
Thrilling
Tidiness
Time
Timeliness
Tolerance
Tradition
Tranquility
Trust
Trustworthiness
Truth
Understanding
Unflappability
Utility
Valor
Variety
Victory
Vigor
Virtue
Vision
Vitality
Warmth
Watchfulness
Wealth

Winning
Wisdom
Wittiness
Wonder
Work
Youthfulness

Keeping Up With Karl

Author: Karl W. Palachuk is the author of several books for technical consultants, including *The Network Documentation Workbook*.

A Bifurcated Guy: Karl leads two lives, in a sense. One is the business owner for three companies in Sacramento, California. The other is a trainer in the philosophy of Relax Focus Succeed®. Doing this successfully takes balance, which seems appropriate.

Trainer: Karl has been teaching in some form or other since 1983 when he became a teaching assistant at the University of Michigan. He taught college for ten years.

These days he puts on seminars for Relax Focus Succeed® as well as business consulting and technical trainings. In all, Karl averages twenty seminars a year.

Blogger: Karl's "Small Biz Thoughts" blog is found at http://smallbizthoughts.blogspot.com. It provides advice for the Small Business owner and manager. This blog has been published since February 2006.

More recently, Karl started an RFS Blog at www.rfsblog. com. That, obviously, deals with the topics found in this book, and is a supplement to the RFS™ newsletter.

Newsletter Writer: Karl publishes three regular newsletters. The first, `Readme.txt`, is for his technical consulting clients. It is produced as a paper newsletter, mailed every month. This newsletter has been published since 1995.

Karl's second newsletter is the Relax Focus Succeed® email newsletter. Published monthly since 2002. That free newsletter is the basis for the Relax Focus Succeed® web site.

Web Sites: Karl manages four primary web sites, plus many others for special projects. For his consulting business, he produces www.kpenterprises.com. That site is not a bland five-page brochure. It is filled with information and resources, and does a good job of attracting new customers.

www.i5pc.com is 25% customer focused. Because it's easy to remember, Karl uses that one in his radio advertising. It has links for all the handouts mentioned on the radio. The other 75% is dedicated to resources for technical consultants.

www.GreatLittleBook.com is the site for the Great Little Book Publishing Co., Inc. The "GLB" site features the books and CDs produced by Karl and his staff.

www.RelaxFocusSucceed.com is just what it sounds like: a place to read newsletters and lots of articles on the philosophy of Relax Focus Succeed®.

Email List: The Great Little Book email list is found at GreatLittleBook.com. This list covers upcoming events, seminars, news, and "what's happening now." Free, of course.

Speaker: If you are interested in having Karl present to your group, or do a training at your office, please contact him:

Karl W. Palachuk
Relax Focus Succeed®
PMB 345
2121 Natomas Crossing Dr. #200
Sacramento, CA 95834

Email: karlp@relaxfocussucceed.com